Careers After 40

App Yourself!

Ron Harding

ISBN: 978-1-4669-8568-1 (sc)
ISBN: 978-1-4669-8567-4 (e)

Trafford rev. 03/12/2013

www.trafford.com

North America & international
toll-free: 1 888 232 4444 (USA & Canada)
phone: 250 383 6864 ♦ fax: 812 355 4082

About the Author

Ron Harding is an award winning author of two books. He has been a contributor to *Advertising Age* and *Business Week*. Harding has been profiled in *The Boston Herald* and *The New York Times*.

He served as Supervisor at Procter & Gamble for nine years and Director at Gillette for twelve years.

Additionally, Harding has been an advisor to nine Fortune 500 companies, career counselor, copywriter, entrepreneur, film critic, lecturer, marketing director, motivational speaker, small business consultant and voice-over announcer.

For twenty three years he has been Professor of Communication and Marketing at Boston University, Curry College, Emerson College and Northeastern University. Harding received *The Distinguished Teaching Award* in 2011.

He is President of Harding & Company, a management training and career development center for eighteen years.

App Yourself!

Your Skills...New Careers

Ron Harding

Preface

For those forty and older, "App Yourself!" is your road map to a successful future. Whether you have lost a job, or are looking for a new career that better uses your talents, "App Yourself" has been written to help you focus on your existing talents and market them in today's competitive market.

Job loss is perhaps as devastating as a divorce or the death of a spouse. I know because I have experienced both. My struggles in dealing with an unexpected firing lead me down several paths, none of them successful. This allows me to speak personally to you about my failures and my successes. I now have five careers going simultaneously, all of them based on past experience and new ways to market myself.

I began career counseling with friends in my church who had lost their jobs because of age, off-shoring or new software programs that eliminated their position. Finding I had a knack for this, I began to formalize a program that investigated their personalities, talents and work history.

Using this program, I began working at it professionally. To date, over one hundred people have found new jobs with my counsel, in three to seven months. They include a part time polyurethane worker who became a designer of guitars for internationally known rock artists, a truck driver who became a successful pastry chef and supplier to some of the finest hotels and restaurants, a free-lance middle manager who signed on as a consultant to one of the nation's biggest wireless telephone companies, an athletic coach at a small college who nearly doubled her paycheck by working as a salesperson for a large rehabilitation equipment company.

As successful as they became, most also point to their personal enhancement in renewed energy, passion for what they do, full use of their talents and greater self esteem.

Future career success is based on a simple idea. That is, the work experience, skills you already have are transferable to at least six other career paths. You don't have to keep sending out resumes, get additional training, or go to 'job fairs.'

What you need to know is that the marketplace has changed dramatically as have ways of marketing yourself. This book will help you re-examine your personality, your marketable skills and show you how to meet with decision makers who are eager to hire right now.

Read on…

Table of Contents

Preface

1. Your First Job   Pages 3-6
2. Loss and its Many Faces   7-11
3. Leading From Strength   12-15
4. Hemisphere Matters   16-24
5. Dishwasher to Recording Artist   25-29
6. How Others See You   30-35
7. C, S and I People   36-38
8. An Inventory of Your Skills   39-41
9. What's Your Passion?   42-43
10. Blue Sky Thinking   44-46
11. A Rich and Satisfying Life   47-50
12. Preparing to App Yourself   51-52
13. App Yourself   53-55
14. The Information Interview   56-59
15. C, S and I Success Routes   60-64
16. Some Success Stories   65-69
17. From Bartender to Hospital Manager   70-72
18. Secrets For A Successful Interview   73-80
19. References, Salary Negotiations and Contracts   81-84
20. Entrepreneurship   85-87
21. Company Size and Growth Opportunities   88-92

Your Personality

Your Personality

1

<u>Your First Job</u>

How did you find your first job? Chances are your family played an important role in that decision making. If you were the first born, the family's hopes, social status, real or imagined, were riding on you. From the earliest years, the first born are given to understand they are responsible for carrying forward family values, establishing themselves in a position that has a sense of importance both to the family and relatives. Were you the first born? You probably found yourself being interviewed by some mature friend of the family. You were treated like an adult, expected to achieve some prominence in a chosen field. (http://suite 101.com/article/does -birth-order-affect-your-personality-a241455)

You were expected to be conservative, follow orders, play by the rules. Many first borns are given little choice, often being expected to fulfill unrealized dreams of their parents. Sociologists call these 'inner directed people' meaning that the voice of a parent forever echoes in the mind. All the attention showered on you made you ambitious, responsible and yet measured by someone else's expectations. The downside of this attention is that your own creative choices were limited. You may have developed perfectionist standards in attempting to measure up, and given in to bouts of anxiety about performance. The loss of a job, especially for the first born, carries with it a feeling of 'a fall from grace.' Men especially lose more than a job. They lose self esteem. Often their personality and their job title are self identifying characteristics. It is not just economic dislocation, it is a personal reappraisal. This reappraisal tends to focus on self imposed limitations. Supposed short comings in personality loom larger than a genuine inventory of skills, aptitudes, experience, positive characteristics and ingenuity, all the proven capabilities you have worked so long to establish.

Does this sound like you?

If you are the second born in the family, the older sibling represents a given path you may wish to avoid.

The second child sees the first born as 'competition' for their parents attention and will set goals for themselves that may be in direct opposition to where the first was directed. First born an 'intellectual type? Second born may want to succeed in sports.

The second born child is probably a better read of family dynamics, often siding with one parent, then the other. Second borns may be 'smoothers' inside the family or overtly aggressive. They will tend to be more influenced by their peer group than their parents. They probably are greater 'risk takers,' and are 'outer directed people.' Outer directed people want group acceptance.

This can well promote anxiety. In his book <u>The Lonely Crowd,</u> Harvard sociologist David Reisman, refers to this group as 'radar people,' constantly sending out signals to their desired peer group, to discover what the group feels about current issues: politics, sexual ethics, abortion rights, authority figures.('The Lonely Crowd' David Riesman, with Nathan Glazer and Reuel Denny,Yale University Press,1961, pages 24,25)

Without the restraints imposed by relatives, organized religion and traditional values, they are more suspicious of rules, laws, and established institutions. Think of recent demonstrations against Big business, Wall Street, Government. How many are second borns? They are certainly acting out 'group think.'

Does this sound like you?

If you are the third or later born, you will probably be given a greater set of options. You are the 'baby' of the family, as much raised by your older siblings as your parents. You may be one of the 'latch key' kids. You are less predictable, often affectionate. You may also be more manipulative, less likely to accept blame and given to immature behavior.

Your approach to work is more adaptive. You are pretty sure 'something will come along.' If not, moving back in with the family is always possible. You are, after all, the baby of the family.

Does this sound like you?

Ask yourself where you fit into this equation. Now ask yourself whether your parents urgings set the dynamics for the job you first landed. Given your current analysis of your past, is this the job you would have picked for yourself?

What probably happened was that you were successful in your first or second job. You used those skills the job demanded. In a very real sense, you cut your expectations to be a good fit for the job you ended up with. You got married, had kids, gained more expertise in that job you were ushered into.

About age forty-five, you may have had a real wake-up call. You were fired, divorced, brought up short. Some like to call this "a mid-life crisis." What it really may be, is a time of taking stock of where you are now. You suddenly realize you are not going to live forever. Your parents may be dead or you're supporting them. You still have a long way to go in your working life and you may be asking yourself, "How did I end up here? Do I want to do this for the rest of my life?"

Why fired? You probably think it was something you did or said. Most of us somehow feel being dismissed was at least partly our fault. We internalize damage and blame. Our vision of the world at large is compromised by events.

Only in retrospect do we begin to consider forces outside ourselves may have generated job loss.

It may be you reached the top of your earning potential and your future retirement and health benefits alerted some Financial Controller inside the company that the longer you remained on staff the more likely your retirement or health benefits would be costing the company future profitability.

Firings in the 1970's began hitting those fifty and older. By the 1980's, more dismissals wre being enacted on those in their late forties. According to job counselors and talking with friends, firings now begin during employees most productive years, ages forty-two to forty-six.

The acceleration rate came coupled with more women in the work force and the annual arrival of college graduates, about one million plus each year. These young people have up to date skills, are eager to prove their worth, willing to work on their own time, evenings and weekends. They can be hired for a fraction of what those 40+ are making.

The thing they don't have is work experience. Nor have they developed a sense of team work and genuine management skills. What they do have is excellent networking skills and little sense of loyalty to any employers. They are 'on the make.' Get a job here, leverage it to land there. They are agile as mountain goats.

You, forty or older, face the new workplace mentality. According to the Bureau of Labor Statistics, the average job life span now at any company 3.3years. (http://bls.gov/news.release/archives/jolts_03132012 htm March 13,2012) Everybody is temporary! That includes CEO's, middle management and factory workers. Throw into that mix the hiring of temporary workers in India, Pakistan, the Philippines, all willing to work for a fraction of their US counterparts, and you have a good feel for why job hunting is so difficult.

So, what is required of you to get a jump on all this competition? First, the realization that you have been time tested, that you do have solid work skills, that you are a unique, independent, mature individual with capabilities no one younger has.

As I have nurtured your generation, given them valuable insights, new ways to explore the job market, I am always impressed with the maturity, sense of values and character traits that come only with maturity. Part of my sessions are spent on helping them and now here, helping you, re-discover your individuality, respect for your working skills, life experience and a wealth of characteristics that are admirable, desirable and durable. As someone once put it: 'God doesn't make junk.'

I always leave my meetings with a certain sense of wonderment that people who consider themselves 'ordinary' are really such extraordinary people. Some clients I have worked with call me 'an encourager.' That is part of my nature. I learned it from my Dad. I consider myself blessed that I have the opportunity to draw on their vitality, become part of their fulfillment, help them fuel their passions for new, rewarding careers. Life is a journey of purpose. When I say my prayers, I include all of them for giving me a purpose to keep going and thankful that so many keep in touch to tell me about their success. They empower me. What a wonderful experience that is.

What we're about to do now is to help you re-imagine your unique skills, to discover how your individual talents set you apart from other job seekers and to restore your sense of individual worth that may have disappeared with the job you lost, or walked away from, because it was sheer discouragement to keep going to that job, just to put food on the table and pay your monthly bills.

You have more opportunities to find a fulfilling career and one that may pay you more than ever before. What you need is a roadmap to future success. This is it.

Job seeking has changed with technology. Old patterns like sending out a resume to companies you see on-line or in ads in the newspaper seldom work. I'll tell you why.

Networking does work. But only with the right people. LinkedIn is mostly set up for people advertising themselves. What you need is being linked up with decision makers who are looking to hire. I'll tell you how to find them in this book.

App Yourself is about what works to get you hired in today's job market.

2

Loss and It's Many Faces

The loss of a job and the search for a new one comes on the heels of disappointment and depression. Some mornings you barely have the strength to get out of bed. Loss of a job is very similar to the death of a loved one, or a divorce. Whether you have lost a job or considering moving in a new direction, you have been under an enormous amount of pressure. Loss of familiar faces at work, loss of a familiar schedule, loss of income, loss of social status, all these contribute to a lost sense of direction, hope and the question, "Will I ever be able to reclaim a part of what has been taken away."

These feelings need time to work through, perhaps as long as a year, maybe longer.

At the same time, you have probably gone through a period of soul searching, prayer, perhaps anger at God: "How could this happen to me? Where were you when I needed You most?" This is a dark time of the soul.

Soul searching is really a personal investigation of who we are, but too often only an inventory of our weaknesses. But you are doing this at a low point in your life. Self recrimination is a natural phase through which we pass, must pass, until we gain a more realistic appraisal of who we are.

During this time, home, our sanctuary, may feel like a prison. Get out. Take a walk. Go to your church, synagogue, mosque. Stay with people who affirm you.

Remember the people around you, your wife and children are hopeful for your success, your return to that positive person you were before. They too are going through this period of suffering along with you. Include them in your feelings, thoughts, plans.

It may be helpful to remind them and you, that this is a period of transition. If your temporary situation means cutting down on household expenses, please explain this to them. Enlist their support. It doesn't mean the kids will never go to college. It may be they get a student loan or get a job. Facing reality means coming to terms of what is, not necessarily some dream you had for the future.

All is not lost. The future will find you and your family in a better place. Wounds do heal over time. But healing takes its own time. Energy does return. New options for new work come with time.

Give yourself time to release the pressure. Learn to forgive yourself.

If you have detected old patterns that are self-destructive, like alcohol or drugs (pharmaceutical as well), get group support. If you have always carried the responsibilities of the only child, or being the second or third child, recognize that your first allegiance is to yourself. Stop trying to live up to someone else's expectations.

As you have lived through this dark time, begin to look at yourself with new eyes. By that I mean put aside old disappointments, angers, fears, self recrimination. Stop playing those old tapes in your head. Whenever they begin to play, say "No!" out loud if you must. Why? Because all those moments filled with 'could of, should of,' are in the past.

Set expectations for what will make you happy, revive your passions for what you want to become. Be prepared to examine new options. You have a vast reservoir of experience, skills, and tangible work assets that can assure you of a bright future.

Let me share with you the experience of a young woman who allowed me to work with her. She has given me permission to tell her story in her own words. Read with some care the stages she went through in her journey to self reappraisal and opening herself up to new possibilities with skills she already possessed.

Her name is Leah M:

"My past career was as an athletic trainer. I started off working in what is known as a high school outreach position in which I worked at a physical therapy clinic in the mornings as an aide and then at a local high school for the afternoon/evening. After 2 years, I decided I wanted to move on and get a Master's degree. I attended the University of Pittsburgh and earned my Master of Science in Sports Medicine. While doing this, I worked as an on call athletic trainer, a technician at a Gold fitness Center and finally a clinician at the same Gold fitness Center. Upon graduating I accepted a job working for a minor league baseball team. This brought me to ***** College where I worked as an assistant athletic trainer and also taught classes in the Physical Education department. After about 3 years or working 6 days a week, for minimal pay, no thanks, and being passed over for a promotion, I enlisted the help of Ron Harding.

In my first meeting with Ron, if I remember everything correctly, he asked me some very simple questions about what I had done up until that point in my career. We also discussed my interests, family background. I was given a skills test and a small homework assignment to assess my personality.

In the second meeting, we went over my test results. They came back as being mostly Left Brain Dominant (24) with a strong Right component as well (16). My personality tests came back as I and S. Aside from the results that were provided what I also gained was a huge boost of self confidence. After being passed over for a promotion, I had been down in the dumps...not to mention the 6-day work week and the struggle to make ends meet. I reached a point in my life where I knew I needed to make a change.

Ron provided me with a list of possible careers that suited my personality and skill sets. Some of these included personal trainer, athletic director, entrepreneur, sports broadcaster, youth group director, tour guide and recruiter.

I was immediately drawn to sports broadcasting. With Ron's guidance and instructions I set out to make contacts in the industry. I knew one person, though not the most reliable, who gave me a name at NESN. I was never able to make contact and found other similar efforts to be fruitless. As usual I picked one of the more difficult industries to get into...I do love a challenge, as I knew and confirmed by my personality testing.

I am now working in medical device sales. I work for a company right now, but as I establish myself, I will work as an independent sales person, allowing me to see the results of my hard work in the form of commissions and bonuses (money does make the world go round). Before taxes and work expenses, which are are a bit more compared to athletic training, I received $11,000 a year more in salary.

Throughout the interview process, and now when dealing with clients, I utilize the advice I was given in my sessions. I can't ask a doctor or orthotist to buy my products outright. Instead, it's asking them questions: 'How they do business? Who do they typically see for patients? What are their biggest challenges?' It reminds me of the idea of never asking for a job. Instead I ask for advice on that industry. Everyone likes to feel as though they are important and that people want to help them out. I use those philosophies in my current position.

As stated before, other than sound networking and career advice, I got a personal boost from my sessions. I had reached a point where I wondered if I was ever going to find anything different, or if I had reached the end. I had been through 2-3 years of difficult job experiences causing my personal life to follow suit. I tell everyone that I went to career counseling and therapeutic counseling all at the same time. My sessions with Ron gave me the skills to find a new career and the belief that I was, in fact, worth more than what I had currently. I have complete confidence that if my current position doesn't work out I will have no problem finding something even better, because of everything that I gained during my time with Ron."

Lea's testimony of our time together and her ability to refresh herself in her own mind reflects the joy I feel with all those who have had the faith in me and themselves. The number now is over one hundred. What I have discovered along the way is that we are all in this together. I had a mind changing dream some twenty-five years ago. I still remember it vividly. I was in a dugout canoe floating down a river. The dugout was moving just a little faster than the people walking on the steep slope above me. Some women were carrying baskets on their heads, some were leading animals. It occurred to me I was in Egypt, floating down a tributary of the Nile. My fear was that this rough hewn canoe might tip over. I am not a good swimmer. What took away my fear was that the people on that high upper bank were waving at me. It gave me courage to stand up and wave back. A sense of peace and joy enveloped me. The realization that we are all moving through time together and that the world is a welcoming place changed my outlook and my life. I became a teacher, not just teaching classes, but becoming a mentor for my students long after college. I consider it a privilege when they contact me, telling me about their marriage, children, careers. I sometimes joke that I will only die when God has used me up. Since I'm still going strong (at age seventy-six), with eight careers behind me, it appears that some force other than my own is helping me along.

The 'Test' Lea referred to is found in the next chapter. My hope is that it will lead you to a better understanding of your worth and skills.

3

<u>Leading from Strength</u>

Unique as our fingerprints, every person reflects specific work characteristics. These skills, acting in unison, position us for success in many areas. We utilize skill sets, a combination of brain wiring and experience, every day of our working lives. Because of daily use, limited only by the rules set down by the demands of the job, we often overlook the rich combination of possibilities that might flourish in a different environment.

When others say we have 'a knack' for something, it is their recognition of our special talents. We, of course, take them for granted, often dismissing their value because our utilization of these skills seem so natural and easy for us. Truly said, we are overlooking and minimizing our own gifts.

The old saying that 'we only use half of our brain power' is false. What is true is that our working talents depends importantly on which areas of the brain we utilize to accomplish working goals.

I began research on a book about the brain years ago. I am fascinated by its complexity and its ability to adapt to the tasks we assign it. My hope was to produce a book in laymen's terms, on how the brain accomplishes the myriad tasks we silently ask it to perform each day. By no means an expert, I had researched and talked with doctors who specialized in this area. This was two years before my wife Jean was diagnosed with brain cancer.

Standing beside the surgeon who was to operate on her, he pointed to the place where the tumor rested and gently explained his plans to remove it. "But that's in Broca's area," I said with some trepidation. "Will this operation affect her ability to speak?" The doctor looked at me. "I think that possibility is minor," he said. With proper apologies on my part, "I'm an amateur, but I do have some understanding," I think I said, the surgeon and her doctors allowed me to look at MRI's and CAT Scans on her progress.

I cannot say enough good things about the team at Massachusetts General Hospital, doctors, surgeons, nurses, who were not only expert, but warm and caring, seeing me through this trying time as much as my wife. Jean survived and became the wonderful woman I had married twenty years before. Unfortunately, the cancer returned five years later. This time, the doctors with all their skills, could attempt only palliative methods.

With dedicated hospice workers, I now assumed the role of amateur caregiver. Jean died at home. She was a fighter, survivor and great companion till the last. As long as I live, a special part of my brain still holds her sweetness and laughter intact.

You may remember Lea M's comments on the results of the simple test I gave her in our initial sessions together. She laughed as I explained the skill sets her test revealed.

"You got me!" she said, somewhat surprised at the verification of her own thought processes.

As you take the test, you may find it similar to tests you had in high school, the ones that were given for IQ, (Intelligence Quotient) or other tests that attempted to highlight where your brain gave a readout of areas in which you showed your greatest facility.

Because those tests were given early, they do not reflect the experience you have at your disposal now. So please take the simple test that follows, with the understanding it will help us both gain perspective on your special talents and the ability to lead from strength in your future career search.

If you find some questions where you are undecided, ask your spouse, significant other, children, friends or co-workers for their insights on what answer you should circle. They may know you better than you yourself.

Take your time. Have fun with it. The best part is that there are no wrong answers!

Test

1. I seldom daydream   yes   no

2. When I listen to music I   listen for tempo   see pictures

3. I am considered a perfectionist   yes   no

4. My house is   something of a show place   comfortable

5. I kick a ball with my   right   left   foot

6. I would rather   lead the parade   design a float

7. I hold my fork in my   right   left   hand

8. I like my work day to be   scheduled   unscheduled

9. I write with my   right   left   hand

10. On vacation I   make a list of things to do   make it up as I go along

11. I like to be   dressed for the occasion   comfortable

12. When I cross my arms my   right   left   hand is on top

13. The world would be a better place if   people followed the rules
    people were more considerate of each other

14. I would rather be a   writer   painter

15. I prefer to work   with others   alone

16. I am considered a   team player   talented individual

17. I would rather take on problems   one at a time   work on several at a time

18. I am a better   problem solver   visualizer

19. When I listen to people I turn to them with my   right   left   side.

20. Work problems can be solved by   seeing what has worked in the past
    coming up with some new ideas

21. I frequently look at my watch or clock   yes   no

22. I am better at remembering   names   faces

23. I would rather learn the   piano   violin

24. I would rather see a   movie   play

25. I am a list maker   yes   no

26. When it comes to law enforcement there is   too little   too much

27. If I decide to landscape my front yard I   measure it out   eyeball it

28. When I meet for lunch I   am punctual   try and make it on time

29. My office is   neat   has piles of stuff around

30. If you want a job done right   do it yourself   take the time necessary

31. I prefer   predictability   spontaneity

32. A boss should   take charge   gain a consensus

33. When I talk to people I   am guarded   let it all hang out

34. When I go to the mall I   get in, get out   browse around

35. When I use the phone   I have a purpose   I chat

36. Promotions go to people who   work hard   know the right people

37. I prefer things to be   in their proper place   in attractive groupings

38. On a project I want   specific guidelines   the ability to contribute

39. At the beach I   take a book   just enjoy the day

40. Looking at this test I   could have done it better   guess it's ok

Scoring

Count the number of questions with the first answer circled. Count the number of questions with the second answer circled. Count the number of questions left unanswered.

In the next chapter, we'll look at the insights your test reveals, to help you lead from your working strengths.

4

<u>Hemisphere Matters</u>

If the number of questions with the first answer circled are highest, you are most likely a Left Hemisphere person. If the number of questions with the second answer circled are highest, you are probably a Right Hemisphere person. If you left more than five questions unanswered, you are more likely a Right Hemisphere person. If your answers are almost evenly split between first and second answers circled, you are a Whole Brain thinker. (About five percent of us are). Congratulations!

About eighty-six percent of us are Left Brainers, i.e. right handed. Nine percent of us are Right Brainers, i.e. left handed.

Let's be clear. No group is less accomplished than the other. What this simple test is meant to reveal is the area you rely on most to accomplish daily tasks. This is usually 'wired in," by the time we are seven. The other hemisphere may be seen as 'complementary' to your primary work station. It applies additional support as a 'backup system,' frequently becoming active when we sleep.

Let's go back now and review the questions and your answers to this brain 'road map.'

1. To a LBD time is money. RBD enjoy letting the imagination run free with no specific goal in mind.

2. LBD are numbers people. Listening for tempo is an exercise in arithmetic logic. RBD use music as a launch pad for freeing the imagination.

3. LBD seek perfection in all they do. They sometimes find themselves thinking about finished projects and how they could have been done better. Even when they are congratulated about a piece of work, they may say (if only to themselves, "It could have been better"). RBD tell themselves, "Well, that's done."

4. LBD take pride in their possessions and use it as validation of their work ethic and status. Frequently done by a designer, the home of a LBD is tasteful, stiff and may have the look of "not being lived in". RBD much prefer flow, with artfully done alcoves of pottery, paintings or plants. Lighting tends to be more dramatic to highlight areas of special interest. The effect is one of personalization and warmth.

5. If you kick a ball with your right foot, you are a LBD. Kicking a ball with your left foot, you are a RBD. If you kick a ball with your left foot but write with your right hand, you have been re-trained at some time in the past from one hand to the other.

6. If you would rather lead the parade, you are indeed a LBD. You like to be recognized and to take charge. If you would rather design a float, you are certainly a RBD. This allows you the chance to use your spatial gifts as well as color.

7. Which hand you hold the fork in is again the dominant hand. Most Americans hold the fork in their left hand to hold food as they cut, but then switch the fork to the right hand to eat. Many Europeans continue to use the left hand to slice and cut and continue to eat with the fork in that hand.

8. Liking your work day to be scheduled is a trait of the LBD. Having the day be more free-form is compatible with RBD.

9. Since the brain and body is wired in a cross lateral pattern, LBD usually write with their right hand, RBD with their left.

10. On vacation if you compile a list of things to do and try and hold to a schedule, you are LBD. If you just make it up as you go, you are exercising the prerogative of a RBD, who tends to go with the flow.

11. Dressing for the occasion and checking ahead to see what people will be wearing is the mark of a LBD. The key here is fitting in, a dictate of the office. RBD tend to wear what they like, seeing they were invited, not their clothes, and then wearing what seems right to them on that day.

12. When you cross your arms, the dominant hand always crosses to land on top. It is the active hand. If your right hand is on top you are a LBD. Left hand on top, a RBD.

13. LBD are rule followers, logical thinkers. Rules mean order. RBD believe rules should bend to circumstance and allowances should be made for people, depending on the situation.

14. LBD like to deal with written words. RBD prefer to express themselves with pictures.

15. LBD prefer to work as part of a group, exhibiting their competitive skills. RBD prefer to work independently, to be at one with the material, in order to better shape it.

16. Being seen as a team player, in spite of the competitive will to win, is what causes many LBD employees to become internally anxious and depressed. The RBD wants to be recognized as a talented individual and expects to be rewarded on the basis of individual achievement. When a superior takes credit for the work, as often happens in a business setting, the RBD takes this as a personal affront and will often work to embarrass that superior at a future date.

17. LBD prefer to work in a linear fashion, one problem at a time. This permits them to give full attention to the work. Since most executives are confronted with multiple problems, they "prioritize them," i.e. put them in a sequential order of what must be accomplished first, second, third. This permits them to work on a single problem at a time while saying they are working on all.
RBD like to work on multiple problems simultaneously. Not particularly well organized, they will work on one problem as long as it holds their attention, or they run into some mental impasse. They then go to work on another problem. This lack of sequential patterning helps give them time to be inventive and to let the intuitive hunch enter their mind.

18. LBD are inherent problem solvers. RBD are visualizers.

19. People instinctively turn their dominant side to listen to another person. LBD turn to the person talking with their right side, RBD turn to the person speaking with their left.

20. LBD are traditionalists. With a sense of linear development, company history provides a sense of permanence and a track record of what worked and what didn't. This is not only logical thinking, but sound thinking. Many problems are cyclical in nature. By discovering what has worked before, an answer may be quickly discovered and with a few "tweaks" made to work again. RBD much prefer to find new solutions to problems. These may be fresh, innovative solutions. They may also be very time consuming, with the final answer "reinventing the wheel."

21. LBD truly believe "time is money." They are inveterate clock watchers. Because they are strong on scheduling, they frequently 'overbook' their day to make sure the day is crowded. This causes unintentional delays which the LBD will generally resent and treat with irritability, and a demand from staff members that they make "better use of our time," and "be better organized". RBD book fewer meetings and leave time to "catch up on things" and "kick around a few ideas." Meetings may run for several hours and take on an air of sociability.

22. If you remember names, you are a LBD. Most people are. This is why business cards are so popular. If you never forget a face, you have RBD tendencies.

23. The piano is the instrument of choice for LBD. Key display is linear. The violin requires more spatial involvement which is the strength of RBD.

24. Movies are a two dimensional display whose construction relies on linear development. LBD find both of these constructs to be familiar. Plays are three dimensional and may defy linear construction. Spatial involvement is preferred by RBD as are the dynamics that the play is happening in real time with audience reaction affecting tempo and spontaneity.

25. List making is LBD. RBD prefer to let things flow.

26. Because LBD seek order and are suspicious of others' motives, law and order and enforcement of rules, are preferred to impose control on an exterior universe that often seems random and out of control. RBD see law and order as an infringement on personal liberty, the option of making one's own decisions in the face of uncertainty.

27. Landscaping is an exercise in spatial design. To reduce it to more manageable terms, LBD move to a two dimensional system dependent on numbers (yards, feet, inches). RBD prefer to walk the area and lay out various design elements by eye.

28. Punctuality is an important part in the clock-watching world of LBD. (I once had a one o'clock luncheon appointment with my boss who announced upon my arrival, "You're late." The time was 1:02.) RBD consider time expandable. Meeting for any occasion in the RBD world is an agreement: we'll both be in the same place with a window of thirty or forty minutes.

29. LBD place high value on order and discipline. This is reflected in the neatness of their office. The desk is cleared at the end of business. RBD consider desk, chairs, floor all to be working space and have inevitable clutter, reflecting their spatial desires for personal expansion and several projects going simultaneously. RBD don't like their personal space invaded. Clutter helps keep co-workers at arm's length, usually standing at the doorway, and keeping their conversations short. (This is especially true when RBD have to deal with LBD).

30. Along with perfectionism and a need to get things 'right' LBD believe their somewhat obsessive behavior to be a correct working model. Since the LBD has an interior yardstick by which they measure themselves and others, the best results will always originate with them. Hence the saying, "If you want the job done right, do it yourself." RBD believe the answer is in the problem and given enough time the answer will emerge. Consideration of variables is an important part of RBD thinking. Thus, if you want the job done right, give the brain time to sort through alternatives.

31. Predictability is the key to successful life management for LBD. Spontaneity is the goal of RBD.

32. Because a LBD wishes to reduce variables, they believe they should take charge. LBD always hire people who seem most like them. RBD like to brain pick, hear people out, socialize. They will often pick people to work with them who are not duplicates of themselves. You may hear a RBD say, "Judith seems like kind of a flake at times. But I like the way her mind works." Word of warning here for those who work for a RBD. They often seem to be consensus builders but change their mind at the last moment, thanks to some sudden intuitive insight.

33. To LBD, knowledge is power. This makes them guarded in conversation. RBD feel free to 'let it all hang out,' because they are trying to win you over to their position. Letting you 'inside their head' means explaining a rationale for their decision and hoping you will see the world in a whole new light.

34. If you go to the mall with a clear decision as to what you are there to do and do it as quickly as possible, you are a LBD. RBD are like sponges, open to displays, anything new, anything interesting. They may simply enjoy sitting on a bench and watching other people go by, trying to imagine who they are, what they do, who they are meeting. Actors, as you may guess, are primarily RBD.

35. LBD may appear to 'schmooze' on the phone, but they always have a purpose for the call. RBD have periods of solitude when they don't want to talk to anyone, but when they are in the mood, they chat with no clear purpose or end result in mind. Again, this is part of their socialization makeup, and a way to find out what is new or interesting from another person's perspective.

36. Because logic plays such a part in LBD, they believe hard work is the key to promotion. If the corporate culture also reflects LBD, they are probably right. RBD are more distrustful and frequently more clear-eyed about company machinations. Companies do promote on the basis of who is "in the club," or "the old boy's network." LBD will justify the promotions with the caveat, "They must know what they're doing." RBD will mutter and sometimes quietly rebel against this perceived injustice.

37. Preferring things to be in their proper place reflects a need for order and predictability, always signs of LBD. A desire for attractive groupings reflects the wish for spatial balance and aesthetics, an important consideration for RBD.

38. LBD want specific guidelines as they undertake a project. This provides a checklist or constants for them. It also provides a hedge against anxiety, which is prevalent in most LBD who want to avoid mistakes. RBD prefer projects to be more open-ended so they can bring imagination to bear and leave their original stamp on the finished work.

39. Even during periods of relaxation, LBD feel the need to accomplish something. LBD are task oriented. Taking a book to the beach provides 'something to finish' and also returns them to the comforts of a linear world. RBD like stimulation. They are open to the day, the warmth of the sun, the sound of the surf, the cry of gulls, passersby who may be attractive and interesting.

40. In taking this test, LBD will attempt to figure out the working grid, which in this case is very simple. Having detected it, they will then wonder if they should supply answers that will throw off proper interpretation.

Deciding that would not be the correct thing to do, they will at last begin to rewrite the test if only mentally, to make it more efficient (at least by their standards). RBD will probably have fun with the test, be interested in how it comes out, what it might reveal and have a general assessment that 'it's ok,' meaning that it has no genuine impact on how they see themselves anyway. RBD may take only part of the test, and finish it, or not, at a later time.

Whole Brain thinkers (that is people who use both Hemispheres equally) may take the test and make notations in the margins, doodle on the page, draw arrows between similar questions or note the names of associates who seem to be indicated by a question and perhaps ask them to take the test. Whole Brain thinkers will have reservations about any test, read it later, and perhaps write a summary word on it: GOOD! or STINKS!

Women may find somewhat contradictory or ambivalent results having taken this test. This is especially true for working women who have attempted to "fit in" with a workplace that is male dominated and whose systems favor LBD.

This test has provided only the broadest outlines on LBD and RBD and Whole Brain Thinkers. In the following chapters we will begin discussing the strengths and weaknesses of all three types. There is no perfect type, although Whole Brain thinkers most closely approach the ideal in terms of self-actualization and greatest fulfillment of potential. No one type is better or "perfect." Even Whole Brain thinkers can be nasty or prove less than loyal when the chips are down.

Now you may say, this is all kind of interesting, but what does this have to do with my getting a job and discovering new career paths?

The key here is leading from your strengths. Hemisphere dominance lets you know what efficiencies your brain uses to make best use of your stored knowledge. Comparisons to the brain being like a computer are really misleading. Your brain is a muscle. It thrives on experience. If you play a sport, you know your golf swing or hitting a baseball comes with muscle coordination. Your brain stores that information.

Now imagine you are right handed, trying to play that sport with your right hand tied behind your back. It doesn't work. You are demanding the brain retrain itself. Anyone who has had a stroke has to re-learn simple tasks like speaking, feeding themselves, buttoning a shirt. It is a long, arduous task.

If you are ambidextrous, meaning you use both hemispheres working in unison, you are a Whole Brain person. About three percent of us have that capability. About nine percent of the population is left handed. The majority of us are right handed, about eighty-eight percent. This is the reason most tools are designed to be used by the right hand.

The brain is a miraculous entity, but it has limits. Because we ask it to perform so many tasks simultaneously, the brain shuts down those areas we seldom use. By about the age of forty, our brain has set down grooves to speed the transfer of information. Our abilities, what some call 'skills,' are firmly implanted. Habit leads to better functionality.

Don't think of hemisphere dominance as a limiting factor. Think of it rather as your application center. This is where you lead from strength. You are not going to throw these skills away but rather find new ways to use them along with subordinate skills you have restricted in the past because your 'Job Description' insisted you not use them or asked you to put them aside to provide a more narrow focus.

If you are right handed (left hemisphere dominant), these are your prominent skill sets or primary strengths:

- ✓ **Logical**
- ✓ **Analytical**
- ✓ **Fact oriented**
- ✓ **Objective**
- ✓ **Linear**
- ✓ **Technical**
- ✓ **Conservative**
- ✓ **Detail oriented**
- ✓ **Focused**

- ✓ Time oriented
- ✓ Repetitive tasker
- ✓ Disciplined
- ✓ Structured
- ✓ Planner
- ✓ Scheduler
- ✓ Good with numbers
- ✓ Literate
- ✓ Sequential
- ✓ Problem solving
- ✓ Traditionalist
- ✓ Easily managed

Here are some areas where your Left Hemisphere may be working against your best interests:

- • Rigidity
- • Demanding
- • Self involved
- • Perfectionism
- • Obsessive
- • Compulsive
- • Misses 'big picture'
- • Habitual
- • Overly critical of others
- • Number driven, not value driven
- • Stubborn
- • Intimidated by authority

If you are left handed (Right Hemisphere Dominant), these are your prominent skill sets or primary strengths:

- ✓ Visualizer
- ✓ Conceptualizer
- ✓ Spatially oriented
- ✓ Imaginative
- ✓ Whole picture thinker
- ✓ Sensory
- ✓ Intuitive
- ✓ Non-sequential thinker
- ✓ Creative
- ✓ Idea sharer

- ✓ Spiritual
- ✓ Group consolidator
- ✓ Progressive
- ✓ Empathetic
- ✓ Good with images
- ✓ Promoter of ideas
- ✓ Consensus builder
- ✓ Group organizer
- ✓ Brainstormer
- ✓ On-Site Leader
- ✓ Image Builder

Here are characteristics where you may have noticed you have difficulties in being your best:

- **Difficulty transposing concepts into words**
- **Weak time orientation (missed schedules)**
- **Lack of follow-through**
- **Mood swings**
- **Not detail oriented**
- **Cluttered workspace**
- **Overly sensitive to criticism**
- **Weak budget skills (cost overruns)**
- **Rebellious**
- **Inability to discipline others effectively**
- **Impulsive**

The key to success in repositioning yourself for success is to go with your strengths, minimize, avoid or slightly correct your approach in areas of potential problems.

Don't be discouraged or feel negatively about your self with any of these findings where you're not at your best. We all have them in varying degrees. Remember too, we use both hemisphere every day, just as we use both hands. But one hand always leads the other in daily use. We use both feet to walk, even if one foot steps out ahead of the other. The key to your success in all this is to know yourself better and put your best foot forward.

Most companies are run by left brain individuals who are analytic, sequential in thinking, and want results confirmed by numbers and explanations in writing. It will require your ability not only to perform but reassure people that you represent a unique combination of skills and value for the dollar. Performance and selling yourself must go together before, during and after hiring takes place.

5

<u>From Dishwasher to Recording Artist</u>

Although Steve R. was not a client of mine, I have known him for thirty years. He has made so many successful career changes, I thought I would include him here. Steve R. is sixty, the oldest of three children, married for thirty-eight years, with two children. He describes himself as right-handed but plays professional guitar, indicating ambidextrous abilities (use of Left and Right Hemispheres).

Steve has had at least a dozen careers, among them: clerk, dishwasher, audio-visual supervisor, marketing manager, professional musician, recording artist, designer, and writer. Many of these careers overlapped or were carried on simultaneously. He downplays these unusual career shifts with the observation: "There are certain technical things you need to do the job. I find it easy to discover what they are."

Here is his interview:

I never knew what my parents' wishes were for my future. My mother wanted me to finish college and cried when I quit. So when I got my Master's Degree at Simmons (College), I told her I expected her to be in the audience weeping copiously as I got my degree and she fulfilled that expectation. I was not pushed to become anything at all.

How many careers to date? Too many to mention. I wanted to be like my father more than anything on earth. He was this outgoing, gregarious guy. And when I found out he was a raging alcoholic and ruined every relationship he ever had, that didn't change my desire to be like my father. When he wasn't drinking, everybody loved him. I wanted to be like that.

In spite of my being an introvert, as I was as an adolescent, I changed. I tell people 'everything you see about me, I've been faking it so long, it feels natural.' Because the last thing I want to do is walk up to someone in a room, stick my hand out and say, 'Hi, I'm Steve R.' But I saw my father do it. He did it so he could get an audience and talk about himself…(laughs). But the thing I'd do was say, 'Why are you here?' and then shut up and listen. I developed that skill early, to engage people and talk to them in spite of the fact I was shy and afraid of rejection.

The next thing I found I was good at was just getting things quickly. If someone was explaining a skill, other than physics or math, I would get it, usually before the person was done explaining it. I would become impatient.

In my career I have found that there are certain technical things you have to know to do the job. I find it easy to find out what they are and realize 'I can do that.'

I answered an ad for an experienced floor sander because I had quit school and I needed a job. I had once rented a sander and sanded my mother's floors and butchered them terribly. But it was an experience and I knew that if the guy would just show me, I would get it real quick. So he hired me and we went on a job and he said, 'Why don't you work the edger and I'll work the big machine'. And at a break he said, 'You never sanded a floor before?' and I said, 'Well, I actually did.' And he said, 'You never did it for a living'. And I said, 'That's true.' And he said, 'But I like your chutzpah, so I'll keep you.' So, basically I am not afraid to tackle new things.

And I found out that I wasn't that special. If you take the time to show someone the one or two buttons to push, and they would never know until you told them, 'when this happens, push that button,' anything can be learned.

When I became Manager of the Internship Program at Gillette, I said I could teach anybody anything, because most things are not that hard. So I was happy hiring people to do stuff because I also realize that I like a lot of empty free space in front of me. You know, time to hang out and do stuff…music and/or prose or writing songs.

And I must have a thing for big corporations, because that's where I ended up so much. You know PsychoCybernetics, the Maxwell Maltz book, says, 'People usually get what they think about, what they dream about.' So I had a lot of jobs where I had a lot of free time. You know, none of these jobs where people are saying, 'This is due on this date,' or 'do that.' And these are most of the jobs I went after and got. I did have a few jobs where I didn't have a lot of time to myself…and I didn't like that.

I do like being challenged. I had a boss (at Gillette) who was always asking me to do things, but never telling me how to do it. I didn't like that, but he was always saying, 'You'll figure it out.' And essentially he was right.

I worked at the Gillette Company for twenty-two years: dishwasher, stock clerk, secretary, audio-visual specialist and the last job I basically created on my own, on the Sensor Razor, Marketing Manager. Again, it was easy. Everything is easy.

Basically, if it is hard, I tend not to want to do it (laughs). In fact, I said to a marketing guy once, I was sitting in his office, "I wonder if other people know how easy this is?" And he just stared at me as if I was telling some 'club secret' you're not supposed to be telling anyone.

I am also a musician. I started a little band and I made some money doing that. I made a lot of money with my music while I was still in corporate America.

I needed the money. I think money is a motivator. I think that's why our society uses it. So if I find something I like, I can do it, and people give me money for it, I go about it in a very systematic way: find out who to call, make a few phone calls and get hired.

I went to school several times, did not stick with it several times. But the last time I did stick with it and got the degree. Probably one of the hardest things I ever did was to take that Simmons (College) program and stick with it until I graduated. And the way I did it was four nights of courses a week.

I wrote my thesis simultaneously with my last semester there. They (school officials) were very much against this. As a matter of fact, I was strongly advised not to attempt it, because I had a fifty percent travel schedule at the same time with my job (at Gillette) while I was in school.

But I was focused for that twenty-four month period. I refer to it as the 'atomic bomb thing'. I do everything at once and then I rest.

My primary skills? I'm a writer. And I do know how to introduce myself. When you do that, you know, very many people look askance. They're afraid of you. So sometimes I think my persona comes off a little severe. You know, people have told me that when they first met me, I was kind of frightening. So I've tried to soften that. This is not self-awareness, this is listening to what other people say.

When I come into a situation I don't know, I try to engage with them, the people I don't know. And I'm pretty good at that.

I've been fired many times. The last was Gillette. How did I get over it? I got another job. Every time I got fired it was usually because I had a big mouth and couldn't keep it shut. I was a little inflammatory as a young man and would get into problems that way. So if somebody fired me, I'd say to myself, 'Well, I should have kept my mouth shut on that one.' And I'd move on.

Have I noticed job discrimination because of age? Oh, definitely! When I left the Gillette Company I was 45 years old. Since my children were still in college, I figured I still had to earn some money. My severance or retirement money wouldn't kick in for another five years. So I tried to do what my skill set was at the time, which was corporate visual production, corporate script writing.

I sent my resumé around, pretty good looking resumé too, I thought, and nothing. As a matter of fact, when I left the company I had a few consultants tell me they thought I had an excellent age discrimination case. I said, 'Please, I'm not doing that.' I believe after you reach the age of forty-five or fifty you become much less marketable, because first, you're too expensive really.

And it was really getting too hard to fake it anymore, generating excitement over something not exciting. So I asked Rosemary (Steve's wife) 'Do you think I could just play guitar for a while?' She said, 'Do whatever you want.' And so I did.

As I get older, do I notice a sense of change about myself? Well, sure. A lot of people have noticed the change, especially after I went to AA (Alcoholics Anonymous). And we mature. We begin to see ourselves as others see us. Because after a certain age you become more introspective, I think. I've become a good deal calmer. And she's (Rosemary) become a lot more like me. That's the advantage of sticking with someone for thirty-eight years. You sort of meet in the middle.

Is money or satisfaction more important? I say it's very hard to separate them. I'm a guitar player and I make CDs. I go out with my guitar and I offer my CDs for sale. When they don't buy them it's very hard to say, 'Well, I'm satisfied playing my guitar.' Because at the last show we sold over one hundred CDs and that was satisfying, very satisfying. I don't think you can be satisfied just doing what you like if you're not making a living doing it."

Analysis:

Despite **Steve R**'s somewhat casual approach to describing his career success, there are a number of points worth emphasis.

First, Steve is an **Intrapreneur**. He reinvented himself many times inside the same company thanks to his ability to listen, find out the essentials required for the job, and have clear goals for how he wanted the job to work for him.

Second, as he makes clear, having the chutzpah (nerve) to take on the responsibility of the job works in a person's favor. People are willing to do the 'job training' for someone with focus and the will to succeed.

Third, the basic skills used to master a job are not that hard to learn. As Steve puts it, it's learning which button to push when something happens. Nearly everyone with work experience knows that every company has their own system. The first thing a new college hire hears are the words, "Well, that may be what they taught you in school, but here's the way we do it around here." Every organization has a system that spells out in detail what is expected and the way it is to be accomplished.

Fourth, there must be a match of compatibility, what you want to do and what the job demands. Skills, expectations and personality are the keys not only to satisfactory performance (company standards) but to personal engagement, mastery and self satisfaction (personal standards).

Fifth, behavioral attitudes can be modified or changed when the need to do so becomes apparent. As Steve says, "The last thing I wanted to do was stick out my hand and introduce myself…"

But he became good at it through practice, in spite of his initial shyness and fear of possible rejection.

Sixth, take a hard look at your shortcomings. Steve recognized his father's alcoholism, that it 'ruined every relationship he ever had,' and saw his own problem with alcohol. He joined Alcoholics Anonymous. In looking at yourself, Alcoholics Anonymous stresses its members conduct 'a fearless moral inventory of yourself.' This means an honest recognition of one's own shortcomings and weaknesses, then a rigorous program to overcome them. Steve did.

Seventh, the ability to find satisfaction in your work and make money at it. As he puts it, "I don't know how to separate them. I don't think you can just be satisfied doing what you like to do if you're not making a living at it."

This is what "App Yourself" is all about.

6

How Others See You

We all try and present to the world a personality that is interesting, attractive, appealing and resourceful. We want to be liked, appreciated, unique in some way.

After the loss of a job, we show the face of defeat: apprehension, fear, sorrow, anger.

This is why we need time to let all this play out. You are not defeated. You are exhausted, battered by events over which you had little control. Not only your face but your body reflects your loss.

The expression, 'time heals all wounds' is appropriate but not complete. Wounds leave scars, scars in your memory. It is not until you change mind set: 'that was then, this is now,' does your attitude and personality show meaningful improvement.

Having passed through a terrible time, look at what you still possess: a world of experience, friends who love you, and a talent base only you own. Possibilities still exist, in greater number than you have ever imagined.

'Put on a happy face' is an old song. It is also a truism. When you force yourself to smile at anyone you see, watch their reaction. They smile, nod, recognize you as an individual. Studies have shown that forcing yourself to smile signals your body to send a corresponding posture. You appear to gain height, your shoulders are back, your body relaxes and your breath becomes deeper.

Most likely during this period of decompression, your energy level is low. It is difficult just getting out of bed many mornings because the day ahead may prove fruitless once again. Especially, left brainers experience brain fatigue. I am essentially a left brain guy, 76 Left Hemisphere, 24 Right Hemisphere, which means I tend to follow old patterns hoping for a new outcome. Some people have wisely observed this is similar to going to Las Vegas to rebuild your fortune.

Home may be your place of refuge. You stay there dutifully, going on-line to see what Google, Yahoo or any other search engine may list for job openings. You read the Sunday 'Help Wanted' pages…anything there?

I did this. I also went to Career Centers and spent seven exhausting months with no positive outcome. Having been out of work for six months, I finally applied for Unemployment Insurance. Driving thirty miles to the nearest office, I felt ashamed standing in line to get my check.

How could I be doing this? I had been highly successful in my time at Gillette, twelve years. I had received a five thousand dollar bonus for being recognized as one of the company's "Best Ten Managers" four months before I was fired.

Actually, I wasn't technically fired. I was told my position had been 'discontinued.' Being discontinued is like walking into your office and finding no floor. Mine was on the twelfth floor of the Prudential Building in downtown Boston. I was in free fall all the way to the basement. I was forty-six.

My reputation on the street was a good one. A favorable piece on me had been written in The New York Times, publishing my entire speech given at The Plaza Hotel to some six hundred business people from around the country. Congratulations from my lunch mate, Walter Cronkite, who was to follow me at the lectern, made me dimly aware I had done well. (No one could see the back of my coat was soaked with sweat when I finished).

The Boston Herald was equally effusive after I lost my job, calling me 'The quiet force that helped Gillette shed its 'blue collar' image and turning it into 'a world class marketer.'

With all this going for me I thought, my employment at another company would be accomplished in a matter of weeks. My estimate was off about eighteen months. My daughter was going to college now, so the cash flow out was something I viewed with subdued panic. I was also paying alimony to my ex-wife, who was demanding more money every six months and had me dragged into court to pay her mounting clothing bill and living allowance. Even though I was still paying the mortgage payments on my ex-house, I was advised by my financial advisor to give her a lump sum payment of fifty thousand dollars to settle out of court. I did.

With all this behind me, I soon had no need for a financial advisor. My funds were depleted. My ex died two years later. She left me nothing. She had gone through the settlement in less than two years. (This was in 1989, when money was still worth the paper it was printed on).

I was mentally, financially, spiritually at rock bottom.

I went back to church and there a man I knew fairly well, gave me an exit visa. "You're a smart guy," he said, "why don't you become a teacher?"

I did. I've been doing it for nineteen years. I also wrote a book about advertising during my down time. I'm still using it in current classes I teach at Boston University. It's been translated into three other languages and I'm still getting royalty payments.

The book, "Making Creativity Accountable" is still available on Amazon.com. Unless you are interested in advertising, I don't recommend you buy it.

The moral of the story for all you Left Brainers is simple. I kept hoping my new career path could be built on my old success. I was wrong. The advice of a friend took me out of my rut and paved the way for my survival. Incidentally, I get more personal satisfaction and good feeling about myself teaching than I ever did working at Procter & Gamble or Gillette.

Others may see in you the possibilities you don't. That's why I'm gently nudging you to open your mind and get out of your house.

Left Brainers, and I'm sure some Right Brainers too, can fall into a rut. This is like trying to drive forward while looking into your rear-view mirror. Experience sets down physical grooves in the brain. This is why when things are going well we call it 'being in the groove.' When things are not going in our favor, we call it 'stuck in a rut.'

We may not know much about the brain, but we instinctively recognize its workings.

It is imperative during low ebb that you re-energize your body and mind. This means immersing yourself in new surroundings. (This doesn't necessarily mean moving to a new area of the country, although this may not be a bad idea) but a gentle reminder that wherever you go, you still bring yourself with you. Geographical cures may be illusory. You drop yourself into unfamiliar terrain, which may impose a whole new set of pressures.

Immersing yourself in new surroundings may be as simple as doing new things. Go to a different mall, go to an art museum, take a walk in a public garden. All of this is free.

Be aware of your new surroundings. Soak up the 'right now' experience. It's been called 'taking time to smell the roses.' Again for Left Brainers, we have been trained to be at arm's length from physical sensation. We're too busy analyzing. Enjoying simple pleasures is the business of the Right Hemisphere. Don't you want to give that under-utilized hemisphere time to breathe and flourish? It may pay rich dividends.

Revitalization, change of mind-set, transforms you from the inside out. You feel and you look differently to others who see you. You are a better you.

How we are seen by others has much to do with our personality, the face we present to the world. Personality is pliable. Like actors, we wear certain clothes, speak in a way we find appropriate to the situation, style our hair, live in a place we decorate with pictures, objects, floor coverings, drive certain cars.

All of this is an attempt to show the world how we wish to be perceived. Obviously, situation drives our attempt to 'fit in.' We are social animals. Instinctively, we adapt to place and time, and our relationship with others. There is the You you become with your parents, with your significant other, the character you assume inside your peer group at work and at play.

There is also the introspective You when you are alone and in the privacy of your mind review the day's events and wonder why you made certain decisions or said something that may have future repercussions.

Life experience may be understood to be a series of trade-offs, trial and error. This characteristic works in our benefit, that one doesn't. Over time, we may purposefully shed some elements of our personality because they don't work in our favor, don't exemplify the persona we wish to imply.

How much of ourselves we don't choose to change may be understood as our 'core values,' a line drawn in the sand. Self determination comes with age and experience.

Critical here is 'how much of me do I want to give away' in our daily transactions with others. How much of me am I willing to change to 'fit in' with peer group pressure? How much of me is to be controlled by parents and their hopes through me of status and social standing? How much of me am I willing to give up to fit some company scheme in the exercise of my total talents? How much of me will I give up to please my significant other?

Until now our concentration has been on the Inner You. We've examined the impact of birth order and Left and Right Hemisphere utility. It is time now to look at You in relation to how you handle yourself in such areas as daily social interaction and Job Interviews.

Imagine first you are at a social function. You meet someone you have never met before. You shake hands and say:

_____

_____

_____

_____

_____

_____

_____

_____

_____

_____

Now I'd like you to imagine you are at a job interview. After some small talk the interviewer asks, "So...tell me about yourself." You say:

_____
_____
_____
_____
_____
_____
_____
_____
_____
_____
_____
_____
_____
_____
_____
_____
_____

You now have the opportunity to read how you identified yourself. What qualities were you hoping would exemplify your personality?

How accurately do they support the person you know yourself to be?

I'd like you to write key words you feel most accurately describe the image you attempted to create in the social setting and then the job interview. Under Private, list the qualities you wish you had included in both settings.

Social	Interview	Private

In the social setting, did you identify yourself by occupation or job title? If you did, place the initial C here _____.

Was a large part of your conversation about family and friends? If it was, put an S here _____.

Did you carry the conversation by asking the person you were talking with questions about who they are, what they do, who they know, what sports or teams they root for? If you did, put the initial I here _____.

In the Job Interview, did you state your name at the beginning of the interview? You should have. The interviewer's schedule may have changed (someone may not have shown up and they sent you in instead). This happened to my wife. Saying your name not only identifies you, it also makes the interviewer aware that you wish to be seen as an individual, not just 'the next guy in line.'

Who did the most talking in your last job interview? Who asked the most questions? You or the interviewer? If you can't remember exactly that interview, give your general impression of how it went. Simply state whether you or they controlled the interview session. If the number of questions asked were controlled by the interviewer, write the initial C here _____

If you talked about your family or social organization or hobbies, write the initial S here _____

If the number of questions you asked about the job were as much yours as the interviewers, write the initial I here _____

Now, count up the totals of C, S and I. See which initial seems to dominate.

In the next chapter, we'll explore the personality characteristics that you have found best describe you and the implications for how you stay within your comfort zone as you pursue new career possibilities.

7

C, S and I People

All of us have a basic characteristic with a secondary trait in another category. I am basically a C person, with a strong component of I in my makeup. The C part of me probably explains why I was out of work for such a long time. C stands for Career Oriented or Company people. Association with a career for a long period of time, and the prestige that comes with company recognition, feeds into a sense of stability and safety.

When that position is gone, C people experience a severe jolt of discontinuity. The sense of 'This is Me' disappears with job loss.

C people often depend on their career identity as personal identity. Being narrowly focused, we look for other companies that may replace our former employer. Said simply, we C people wear blinders, like those of a racehorse. Our vision of what else we might do is hindered because we are trained to focus on what we are (were) doing.

What C people crave is continuity, a place to go, a routine to follow, predictability in all things. Remember, a friend of mine suggested a career in teaching. I've been a college professor for nineteen years. So, although my profession has changed, my personality hasn't.

Let's look at some characteristics of C people. See if you recognize some of these traits.

C personalities:

Careful: You seldom take risks or oppose consensus opinions.
Closed: You rarely disclose your feelings, You never reveal your 'game plan' to anyone. You have an office at home that is off-limits to other family members.
Collaborative: You attempt to be a team player, but want personal recognition.
Comfort Seeker: You insist on first-class accommodations.
Committed: You give the company your full attention.
Confidant: You will select a mentor higher up in the organization for advice and support for your own goals.
Conscientious: You apply yourself to the task at hand with total concentration.
Conspicuous Consumer: You enjoy the fruits of your labor and display status through your clothing and surroundings.
Consistent: Your likes and dislikes are predictable.
Controlled: You rarely show ups and downs.
Critical: You seldom give praise but frequently isolate others shortcomings.

C personalities will look for contacts at other companies, primarily concentrating on past business partnerships. Even though cultivating relationships throughout the business world, those contacts are closely aligned with the same category you were in, thus making further connections in other careers limited.

C personalities absorb job loss at a deeper psychological level. Since much of their self-esteem and commitment was localized within the company and their position in it, job loss represents a 'fall from grace'. Typically too, past business associates are only that -- associates. C types may distance themselves from fallen contemporaries quickly, as if job loss represents some sort of contagion. C personalities have greater chances for success if they join another company before the axe falls or if they move quickly before 'word hit's the street'. C types will usually pursue their same career path in another place with total focus.

Now let's look at S people. S stands for sociability. See if some of these characteristics look familiar to you.

S personalities:

Salt of the Earth: You believe in traditional values and systems.
Self contained: You attempt to put on a happy face in spite of pain, disappointment and frustration.
Self-critical: You seldom measure up to standards set by you, your parents, or your religious group.
Self-giving: You give nearly as much priority to others' needs as your own.
Service-oriented: You work best in a group.
Social: You tend to be better friends with one sex. You see people outside the office, give parties for friends and those you work with.
Superstitious: You believe that forces outside yourself may somehow impact on your daily life.

S personalities will talk to everyone about their search for a new job. Acquaintances, friends and relatives will be activated in the search. S personalities may also find greater success by job hunting in teams. S people will also face some disruption in their lives if they lose a job. Work associates are much like a second family. This may also inhibit S people from seeking a new work opportunity of their own volition.

I stands for independent or individualistic. Frequently referred to as 'go-getters' or the 'go to' person, they show a flair for promoting themselves and are also good at networking.

Read these characteristics and see if they help identify you.

I personalities:

Idiosyncratic: You may not wish to follow standard ideas in management and its dictates.
Imaginative: You show diversity in handling problems and creating areas of opportunity.
Imaging: You use visual concepts or word pictures to make your point.
Impulsive: You react at gut level to certain people and situations. You may have a low boiling point. Depending on the situation, you may be a rule breaker or leader.
Independent: You go your own way. You are a realist and pragmatic.
Industrious: You display a variety of skills and have great energy. You frequently have several projects going on simultaneously.
Inspirational: You instill a sense of vision and purpose.
Instinctual: You have a knack for seeing emerging patterns before most others. You are also a good 'reader' of people.
Intelligent: You have superior intellectual gifts.
Investigative: You do your homework on projects. You like to figure out what makes things work.

I personalities, essentially lone wolves, will largely chart their own course. Having met many people and having many irons in the fire, they will make contacts most easily being a natural self-promoter. They may well become a full-time worker on some project they have been working on in a more minor capacity.

Now, please identify your dominant personality and write it below:

_____

Having looked over all the personality types, you will find you share some of the characteristics you possess in another group (C, S, I). None of us are completely one type. **If you find similarities with another group, write it below:**

_____

Consider the first letter as your dominant personality. Consider the second as your complementary or subordinate personality. You may switch to this secondary personality if you find your dominant personality is not achieving the results you wish to accomplish.

Your Skills

8

An Inventory of Your Skills

I am always amazed at the number of skills the people I have worked with possess. Most of them don't realize their own inventory of skills until I coax it out of them. Why? Because we come to see our skills as routine work habits, something done every day.

The general reaction to an enumeration and examination of your skills and the possibilities for new employment using those skills does not quite sink in. "But I've always been a _____. My reply is: 'Up till now.'

Opening your mind to new careers, using your proven skills, takes time. Slowly we begin to discuss where your skills are marketable, what these positions are called in today's marketplace, and how you go about finding and talking with a key decision maker to get that job.

It all begins with a new look at what you already do, have done, and the many opportunities within your grasp. Be prepared to discover the rich vitality of what you already know, talents you have probably overlooked until now.

First, I'd like you to write down your current job title or what you were doing before you lost that job. Write it here _____.

Now, I'd like you to write down a job title that is a better descriptive title for what you have been doing. _____.

Does the second job title reflect what you are really good at? Does it personify you as a working personality? If not, write down a job title or description that seems a better match for your total skill base.

Write it here:

_____
_____
_____
_____
_____
_____

Next, write down the main duties you perform in your current or past job. List all your responsibilities required to be successful in this position. Take your time to think about this. Your responsibilities are:

_____
_____
_____
_____
_____
_____
_____
_____
_____

Now, think of 'associated duties' you are asked to do, or do of your own volition. If you are asked to chair meetings, organize other people's schedules, do presentations, represent your company in some sort of information sessions with outsiders, or take part in screening job applicants, write it all down now.

_____
_____
_____
_____
_____
_____
_____
_____
_____
_____

Which of these associated duties do you like best?

_____
_____
_____
_____

Now, list all the things you hate to do, and want to avoid in your next career.

_____
_____
_____
_____
_____

What would your next career be if you could be anything you wanted and get paid for it?

_____

_____

_____

_____

9

What's Your Passion?

Everyone has a passion for something. What's yours? It may be your hobby or what you do for fun. This has nothing to do with work, simply an irresistible, instinctual pull that occupies your free time. It's involving and provides freedom from the daily business of life. This focuses you on something that even costs money in its pursuit. No wonder some people call it 'a guilty pleasure.'

Write down yours: _____

Some people like baking, others like gardening. Some like baseball and become Little League coaches. Some like to do crossword puzzles. For others, it's going to the movies. Still others like to work on their cars.

All of these are outlets that may have started when you were a child, teenager or young adult. Some of us may have had a childhood hero who was a celebrity or movie star, a comedian or a baseball player.

Who was your childhood hero?

Write it here: _____

Now ask yourself what attracted you to this hero? It may have been their profession, or their look, how they made people laugh, any number of reasons. Try and remember why you were so attracted to this person. Give it a little thought.

Write it here

_____
_____
_____
_____

Did you hope when you grew up you could be like them? Why?

_____
_____
_____
_____

Steven Spielberg saw a Cecil B. DeMille movie, 'The Greatest Show On Earth' when he was eight. He bought a Super 8 camera so he could film his own train wreck with his Lionel train set. (Incidentally, one of his latest movies is called 'Super 8' about children fascinated with making movies. It also contains a spectacular train wreck very much like the circus train pileup in DeMille's GSOE).(James Lipton's Actor 's Studio, You Tube)

Few of us follow our dreams as successfully as Spielberg. But it is his example that should pique your imagination. Childhood is a time when anything seems possible. The sky is the limit. Those dreams never leave us. They just go underground into what psychiatrists call our 'unconscious mind.'

You listed traits of an old hero. You analyzed why you liked them. Now think of you emulating them in a new career. This is a process called 'mirroring.' You assume the characteristics of that person.

Johnny Carson started his career by thinking of his idol, Jack Benny, whenever he went on stage. When the two met later, Carson told Benny the story. "I would never have guessed," Benny said. (The Johnny Carson Show, NBC television)

What Carson did was to emulate Benny, but his individual personality gave him his own style and a lifelong career.

Discover the characteristics of who you admire. Emulate them. Step out of your old persona and into a new one. Just as you take off old clothes and put on new ones, this will freshen your ideas, career possibilities, and point you in a new direction.

10

<u>Blue Sky Thinking</u>

Blue Sky thinking is a chance to let your less dominant hemisphere take over. If you are a Left Brain Dominant, as most of us are, your Right Hemisphere, sometimes referred to as your 'Creative Side,' is never given much of a chance to play a role in your thinking.

Your Right Hemisphere turns on as you sleep. But it still risks being cancelled by your Left Hemisphere. This may be why dreams are stopped…mid dream. What your Right Hemisphere is doing is searching through your neuronal network. Your Left Hemisphere, the analytic, linear, fact oriented side, is trying to shut it down.

Your Right Hemisphere is the door to your Unconscious Mind, that vast neuronal network over which you have little control.

There is a theory that we never forget anything that happens to us. Because our brain is dealing with the present, work, shopping lists, driving Johnny to soccer practice, our daily life demands we stay in the present and the near future.

But the unconscious never stops working. That vast reservoir of memories, smells, feelings, hopes and fears is a random collection of unidentified connections. They may spring up at the unlikeliest time. Hearing a piece of music, you may suddenly remember not only the song but who you were with the first time you heard it, the place, the season, the smells. All of this is buried in your unconscious.

I recently saw an old movie, 'Casablanca' and I suddenly remembered seeing it for the first time at the Kingsland Theater in St. Louis with my Dad. It was a hot summer Sunday afternoon. The show was on at 1 pm. The theater did not have a parking lot so my Dad parked on the street about a half block away. He drove a black Buick. We walked to the theater. It was air-conditioned. This was in 1943. I was seven years old. Now why did I remember that? Pure association. Association is what the Unconscious is good at, if given the time. Ever try and think of an old movie title? You go to Google it and the answer springs to mind before you hit the keyboard.

Why do people go back and see a movie over and over? Because it creates a pleasurable reaction we wish to recapture again. The pleasure center in your brain is an addictive force. Used positively, it generates a sense of well-being. Negatively, it causes problems such as alcoholism, drug use and even depression.

If you connect the dots, you can see how habituation, habits for short, permeates what we do. C types are good examples of this behavior. Having once succeeded in a job we will look for the same job at another company. Being linear thinkers, C types will try again and again, following the same pattern, even when nothing positive results.

The brain sets down grooves of associational behavior, actual grooves in the brain itself. When things are going right we call it 'being in the groove.' When things don't go right we call it 'stuck in a rut.'

Blue Sky thinking happens when you force your mind to stop thinking about daily events. To do this, sit alone, free of distractions. Some people accomplish this by imagining they are in a bare, empty room. The light slowly diminishes until the room is dark. You willfully dismiss any thought that reflects daily life. You will feel a sense of warmth and absolute comfort.

Don't try and call up any memories. Let your mind be a blank screen until something shows up. It may be a flash of an image, helping you find your new career or solve a problem.

Write down the image. Don't try and puzzle it out. The answer will come to you.

Some psychologists call this 'free association.' What it means is that your brain has probably solved a problem like this years ago. Given time to retrieve this answer, the answer will come. It simply can't be rushed or forced.

Companies whose profits are shrinking often ask their employees or an outside consultant to help them 'think out of the box.' Others call it 'brainstorming.' 'The box' is really the company mind-set and its standard thinking.

I heard a story years ago, whether this is factual or apocryphal, I don't know. Here's the story: Now that telephones were in every home and office, no one was buying more phones. So a creative problem solver was called in. On day one, he put a black standard phone in its cradle and an apple on the desk, side by side. His instructions were simple: 'Combine these.' Then he left.

The assembled group was astounded. How could they possibly combine these two dissimilar objects. People began to laugh. Then someone said, "Why does the phone have to be black? Why can't it be red?" Another said, "Or yellow or green? Apples come in different colors."

Someone else said, "What if you cut the apple in half? What if the two halves fit together?" This became the 'touch tone phone' as we know it.

What makes this story useful is that it called upon all the participants to let their imaginations run free. You can do this with friends as you think about new career paths.

Your imagination and your unconscious are treasure troves of ideas. Ideas may come to you at any time. Write them down. Stick them in your pocket. Write them down in this book. Don't allow yourself to dismiss anything.

Have a thought of you stacking milk cartons? Write it down. Look at it next week. It may be suggesting you have management skills or a new career as an analyst. Get out of your own way. Step aside. Dream standing up. Or lying down. Get the juices flowing!

When I have trouble finishing an idea for a chapter, I stop working. I do something that doesn't require much brain power…like cutting grass. Half way through cutting the grass, the solution pops into my head. An AHA moment! I stop the mower, go inside and type. When I'm done, I finish the lawn.

Why do we call this Blue Sky thinking? Remember when you were a kid and looked up at that vast blue vault? Clouds moved by and you made those clouds to be anything you wanted them to be. Remember getting a toy and then using the box it came in as a tank? No one had yet trained you out of childhood dreaming. Get it back!

11

A Rich and Satisfying Life

Carole W. is sixty-four and an administrative assistant and guidance counselor at a college just outside Boston. Carole is an only child, having twin brothers and a sister who died as infants. She describes herself as an S personality with a hint of I. She has had ten jobs in her working life. Although she was not a client of mine, her insights into finding different career paths are invaluable and give a personal touch to everything we have discussed so far. This is her story:

"My parents only wish was that I go to college and pursue whatever I wanted. Neither of them had gone to college. I was a teacher first, which is what I got my Undergraduate Degree in. I taught for the most part sixth grade math. I was a teacher for about twelve years.

Then I became a school social worker for about three years. That took me into student homes as well as doing counseling at school. This was when I was in Dallas (Texas) and that's what I decided I wanted to do. I got my Master's Degree in Student Counseling in Student Services.

I think when I was first going to school, I was trying to decide what I wanted to do. I knew it was either social work or the Peace Corps, or something like that. It was always in me. And when the opportunity came within the school system, then that made it clear.

I became a teacher first because I thought it would take too long to become a social worker. And also tossed into that indecision was, of course, a thought like, 'Gee, maybe I'd like to be a veterinarian. Or run away with the circus'.

I got married and moved from Dallas to Ashland, Massachusetts. They didn't have any teaching jobs. I heard they were looking at Polaroid (an instant photography system) and I heard they paid well, even though I had to work six days a week.

I knew nothing about making cameras and suddenly I was supervisor on a production line supervising twenty to twenty-five people. When I think about it, in a classroom you have maybe thirty or thirty five kids. Now I had twenty adults who sometimes acted like kids. The difficult part when you're trying to manage adults is that they are more strong-willed.

I had never done anything like this, this technical, and I had to know how to build a camera just like they had to know how to build a camera.

I actually enjoyed it. It was interesting and sort of a challenge. I just wanted to show myself I could do it. I had to rely on an awful lot of people who had been doing this for a long time. I had to win their confidence because I was new. And I was a woman and there were only two other women doing the same thing.

There was a little resentment. They were a little cool at first; a lot of them were very cool. But I found that if I went to them and asked their advice, they decided I wasn't too bad. I needed their help. They knew what they were doing because they'd been doing it for years.

I was only at Polaroid about a year because I had the opportunity to go into the Needham (Massachusetts) School system. I started out as a permanent sub. I taught in three different schools, wherever they had openings. I was low man on the totem pole...or woman. I was there about three and a half years until they passed Proposition Two and a Half. So they closed...gee, how many schools did they close? About three or four schools in Needham, laid off about seventy five teachers; those who didn't have tenure were the first to go. So I was fired, which was a big blow to me because I thought I could always teach.

I kept thinking, I won't be fired. This won't really happen because I've been teaching so long. I couldn't believe it when I was fired that this was happening. I just thought, 'What am I going to do?'

It was very depressing. At the same time, my Dad was dying, so it was a double whammy. But it was a blessing in disguise. I was able to spend time in Texas...I would have gone anyway. But this way I could go spend a month at a time with him. It's kind of odd how things work out that way.

And before I left to spend the summer to be with him, I got a call from someone who gave me my next job.

The fellow who ran this small company was a principal who used to be in my school system. It was a small publishing company which was just down the road in Wellesley and it came through another of the principals I worked with. That's how I was referred to this little company.

And, they held the job for me until I came back in September. I was writing children's books, doing text and developing different programs. I was writing, copy editing, proofing, the whole process.

I was there about two and a half years, at the publishing company, and then my husband retired. He wanted to move to the Cape (Cod) and run a Level Four rest home.

I really didn't want to do that, but I didn't have much choice. So I gave my notice, moved to the Cape and ran two Level Four rest homes, which are a level above a nursing home. We did that for about two years and then sold them. I have a real weakness for the elderly and to me it was a very emotional job.

After we sold, I went back to publishing. Actually at two different companies in Boston. I worked at Houghton-Mifflin and another publishing company, there as a free-lancer. Occasionally they'd give you a year's contract. It was a lot more money, a lot more. I mean it wasn't stupendous, but a lot more than teaching and other jobs I'd had.

I commuted on the bus from the Cape to Boston every day for seven years. And that got a little old. Then, oddly enough, a person who was working for Curry College, we commuted together, got a job in publishing. "You know I'm going to have to leave the college", she said. "Why don't you interview for my job?"

I was really sick of riding the bus every day or driving into Boston, so I set up an appointment, had the interview and got the job. I went back into school and my friend went back into publishing. And I've been here for ten years.

My skills? I do think I am sensitive to people. I do like helping people figure out a way to move ahead. I have always wanted to do that. Sometimes I think it's easier for someone else to see what you could be doing than the person themselves. I guess I would say my strengths are empathy and sensitivity and the ability to plan.

As much as I don't like transitions, I am kind of adaptable. I find transitions very stressful, but somehow I manage to do it, so I guess I'm more adaptable than I think.

I do like to think of more psychological reasons for certain behaviors. I find it easy to put myself in the others place, to walk in somebody else's shoes.

I think I'm analytical, logical, but having to 'brainstorm' sometimes, I can do that. I think in some ways I can do both. I don't consider myself really creative unless it's in the kitchen. You asked what hand I use primarily and I was going to say the right, but come to think of it I am ambidextrous. That never occurred to me. How strange.

Age discrimination? I've heard about age discrimination (in the workplace) from friends. And students I've advised, thirty-five, forty, fifty years old have suggested that may have been true in their cases. My husband's friends are not in their thirties, but in their fifties and that has certainly happened. In fact, one of them has an ongoing lawsuit with a company that has been going on for quite some time…years now.

At this stage of life, satisfaction is more important to me than money. I think at this stage of my life I probably think in a more global sense in terms of what's going on in the world.

I worry about it more, probably in the last six or eight years. I also…I do think more about death, coming to terms about what that means. I also wrestle with 'do I want to retire?' If I do retire, what am I going to do, because I've always worked. I might do volunteer work.

Do I have any advice to offer others? Hmmm. I think if you're in a job you really don't like but you're close to retirement, I would say,' hang on', because it's almost like you'd be cheating yourself out of retirement pay and benefits. But find other things to occupy your mind and don't take your job so seriously.

If it's somebody whose job has just disappeared…I have people who come in here and say, 'I look in the papers and there's nothing'. But they're looking for a specific job title as opposed to thinking, 'Gee, I could do this.' List your strengths and categorize them. Then figure out, 'Where do I go from here?'

Don't think so much about your weaknesses. Think of things you really don't want to do, or don't like to do, and apply that to what you're looking for. Like psychology. I have people say 'I never see any ads for a psychologist. And I don't have this or that degree'. And I say, 'Wait a minute!' Psychology is all about human nature and how human beings interact. And that's (the skills used in) Human Resources and employee training. If you just use your imagination in seeing your talents in other settings, you're going to have something that will carry you into that job and you can build on it.

So what it amounts to is getting someone to open their minds and say, 'Gee, what have I always wanted to do and whoops, I have those skills that allow me to do it'. Sometimes it's like creating your own job in your head. Don't pay so much attention to what the job title is. Ask yourself, 'What are they looking for...a leader, a good communicator?' And go with that.

Analysis:

With her abilities as a manager, guidance counselor and teacher **Carol W.** has won the respect of both professional staff and working adults. She advises perhaps ten to twenty people a week: young people entering the job market, adults returning to the work force or going for a higher degree, to position themselves for a greater earning potential.

What **Carol W**. is stressing seems to sum up in different words points we have already discussed:

- **Discover your strengths**
- **Categorize them**
- **Use your imagination**
- **Create your new job in your head**
- **Learn what employers need most**
- **Use friends, colleagues and associates to help you find that job**
- **Be up to the challenge of trying something new**
- **Get more education if it helps achieve your dreams**

Remove the self limits you have placed on yourself.

Replace them with Great Expectations.

Your New Career Options

12

Preparing to 'App Yourself'

You have in hand now a complete inventory of yourself. You have discovered your unique skills, your personality type, your personal strengths, how others see you. It is now time to knit all this information and these insights into a cohesive strategy for success. You know what ignites your passion and what you seek in a new career.

I want you to take a risk, call it 'a leap of faith,' bearing in mind that the job you really want is out there and yours for the taking. Don't limit your options here! You've invested a lot of time assembling your talents, reading this book and seeing yourself as a new person.

Be limitless in your declaration of independence by listing below those 'dream jobs' you've always wanted, confident in the knowledge that what you dream is the first step toward realization of your hopes and ambitions. Tell me what jobs you would take in a heartbeat.

_____

_____

_____

_____

_____

_____

13

App Yourself

So, exactly what is an 'app' and how do you use it? App is short for 'application,' which means an electronic program that can be called up at will. You're probably familiar with it if you have an iPhone.

You know how it works. Hungry? Hit restaurants. Italian food? Hit that. An Italian restaurant near you? Hit that. The way you hunt for food is the same process you'll use to find the job you hunger for.

The key to successful apps rests on specificity. You have to know what you want to get the right information. The same is true of your brain. Much like your phone, your brain needs specific cues to provide the right answer.

The perfect job you are looking for already exists in your brain. What you have to do is to find the right app to call it up.

Asking friends and associates for contacts provides you with names of people you have never met. Even better, their recommendation that you talk to a particular executive serves as their personal belief in your value. They wouldn't be making a contact for you if they didn't believe you had something to offer to the right person.

I call this a 'side door entrance,' because it gets you past the usual people who are not decision makers, rather they are barriers to your success. Include in this number, secretaries, middle managers and Human Resources. These people are 'screens,' meaning they work to purposely keep you from contacting decision makers. However well intentioned they may be, they are stumbling blocks to your success.

These are the people who answer phones, read resumes and sort them. Most of them have no idea what good qualifications are for a particular job. Indeed, many don't even know what the job title implies or requires.

By way of example, let's look at a typical 'administrative assistant' to see how she goes about her task.

Her name may be Candice. She is 24. She listens to music on her iPod. Her job is to screen applicants. She doesn't know what any of these job headings mean. She doesn't need to know. She has nothing to do with hiring. Her job is screening and culling.

Her career day is based on non-selection of candidates. Out of the two hundred fifty applicants that day, she is ordered to select only five. To aid her in the process, the company may use an EDBS (Electronic Data Base Scanner) which speed reads resumes electronically looking for 'buzzwords' or 'reductive phrases.' If you haven't included these in your resume, the system deletes you.

I once met a Candice, looking over her shoulder as she culled. One application looked good to me. "Why is he being turned down?" I asked. "Oh," she said, "our requirements say 'must have five years experience.' He has ten."

Now do you know why your letter of inquiry, resume, application got a 'no response'?

Eighty-five percent of the good jobs, the jobs you want, are never posted. Positions are filled by word-of-mouth.

What this means is that the tried and true practice of answering ads, scanning the Internet, sending off resumes and waiting for a reply, will seldom get you hired.

How many resumes have you sent off? What was the response rate?

The problem here is that once you allow yourself to be flattened into several sheets of paper, no three dimensional You is seen. No conversation takes place. No pertinent questions asked or answered. Even worse, you have probably described yourself in words that reflect the old you, the image you are trying to shed. That position was discontinued, not only yours, but hundreds of thousands like you.

That old job description may be called something else in today's fast paced workplace. Don't date your skills by using a passé job title that has no equivalency in today's market. Don't slap an old label on your marketable skills.

What you need is face to face contact with a decision maker working today. The way you go about this is not to ask for a job but to ask for information about what companies are looking for right now.

Here are the simple steps to successfully 'App Yourself'

- discover your strengths
- write them down
- clarify what you want to do
- use your imagination
- create new jobs in your head
- talk with friends, colleagues, associates to help you make contacts
- discover what specific employers want and need
- prepare for the interview
- meet only with decision makers
- rewrite/update your resume to their specifications
- negotiate contracts, terms and salary

14

The Information Interview

When many of my students are graduating, they ask me how to go about exploring job opportunities. I always suggest they make use of information interviews, by talking with people already successful in their careers.

Now that you have begun the process of discovering one or more career paths that may bring you future success, I am going to suggest you do the same thing: talk with people already established in areas of opportunity.

There is a distinct difference, of course. Instead of a general discussion about what you might do, these interview sessions allow you to talk about skills you possess and work experience. You have established credentials and a new career path in mind. What these interviews are meant to accomplish is the matching of your skills to what is needed to be successful in a new career.

The interview serves other purposes as well. First, it strongly suggests you are looking for a new career opportunity. Second, it allows you to talk about your career achievements and unofficially present your credentials to that decision maker.

Let's be clear about all this. You are not asking for a job and the subject should never come up in this interview session. The decision maker is smart enough to recognize your interest in their area of expertise.

What you are doing is seeking information to see if your established skills may present a good match for what is needed by a company in a particular field. As well, you are learning what title may be attached to that job. As you move ahead, talking with other experts at other companies, your knowledge base will permit you to 'talk their language,' showing your greater expertise in that area and permitting you to stress certain aspects of your past history that seem to indicate you would be a 'good fit'.

What you are implying is that you want to be sure you have the right credentials to be successful in this new career. With the interviewer's assurance you would be a likely candidate, you have placed yourself in that person's memory bank as a potential hire. All of this happens without the pressure of asking for a job now. (There may not be an immediate opening, and you may be surprised by a call from the decision maker several months later.)

Similarly, you may be steered by the interviewer to talk with another person he or she knows, who is looking for a new hire. They will never say this directly. It will usually be couched in a phrase such as, "It might be helpful for you to talk to so-and-so, who may be more helpful in discussing this with you."

The value of information interviews cannot be overestimated. Essentially what you are doing is exploring potential careers by asking advice from a senior player in your field of interest and putting yourself into play as a potential candidate.

Be sure to take notes. This indicates that the person you have been talking with has offered valuable information and that you are listening carefully. Questions about their background, how they entered the field, and what they like and don't like about their daily routine gives you an inside look at the realities of the field and whether you would have a passion for that kind of work.

It also helps you match your skill set with what the career demands. As you briefly discuss your background, you are giving this expert authentic information about you. You are there in person, not a sheet of paper. By asking for pertinent information, you are showing that you understand the mechanics that mean success.

By nodding your head at appropriate times, you are saying with body language that you are familiar with the requirements being discussed.

You may also ask the question, "What kind of job title goes with this position?" You may also ask, "What is the usual salary of a position like this?"

Keep an eye on your watch. The interview should run no longer than twenty minutes. Thank the person for their time. Tell them how helpful this has been. Ask them if they know of anyone else who might also give useful insights.

Often this expert may give you the name of another individual in the field. Ask if it would be all right to contact them.

"Sure," the person may say, "I'll give them a call after you leave so they'll know you'll be calling." This again gets you past the gatekeepers.

You see how simple all this is. Most people want to help. Best of all, with their help, you won't be making a 'cold call.'

Send the expert a 'thank-you note' in writing, not an e-mail. This has three advantages. First, it shows you are courteous and appreciate the time the manager has given you. Second, it reminds them of who they said you should contact. Third, it reminds them of your name, your address, phone number and e-mail contact.

Follow up quickly on your next lead. Take the same steps in this interview as you did before.

Eventually you will get a signal that your current interview is a match for what this company is looking for. You will recognize it if the person you are talking with says something like, "Listen, there's someone else here I'd like you to meet," or "Do you have time to stay for lunch…I'd like to talk with you a bit more…"

Whenever possible, arrange this interview for late morning. If you look like a desirable candidate, you may be asked to stay for lunch, to meet another manager in the company. If this happens, you may be sure you are being seriously considered for a position right now. If an offer is made that day, politely ask if you may think about it for a day or so. This suggests another job offer has been made and you now have the leverage for negotiating working conditions and perhaps a higher salary.

Don't stop asking for another name or contact you might talk with until an offer is made.

Information interviews are the best way I know to get active in the job market and get the opportunity to talk with decision makers.

One last tip: never bring a resume to this meeting. If need be, simply say you are updating your resume, or your new resume is at the printers. You never want to offer a resume until you know the exact qualifications the employer is looking for…and then rewrite it to fit those specific demands.

A good resume highlights your past experience by giving specific examples of your expertise in those areas most sought by the prospective decision maker. Make the resume a written exposition of a specific area.

I have four different resumes for each of my career paths: one for teaching, one for job counseling, another for my work as a voice-over announcer, yet another for advertising/management consulting. Each refers directly to my expertise and track record in that area under consideration by a specific employer.

We'll be talking later about how to use your resume to your advantage during the actual job interview.

Let's look next at how C, S and I types may best use their personalities in Apping Yourself.

15

C, S and I Success Routes

You may wish to look again at the chapter 'How Others See You' to familiarize yourself with your Dominant and Secondary personality strengths.

C types are Career/Company people who believe they have a 'gift' for something and are hesitant to change. C people may also be recognized as Company people who enjoy the prestige of that large entity and gain personal identity from it.

S people are the Sociables who enjoy being part of a group which becomes something of a second family. They usually like to seek others' opinions on what they should do and often operate best as a working unit in seeking new employment.

I are Independents/Individuals with many irons in the fire and are usually referred to as the 'go to guy.' They will be part of a team, as long as their worth is recognized and will arbitrarily jump ship if they are not.

Having reacquainted yourself with your profile, let's examine how each personality type may go about finding routes to success.

Example One:

You have just been fired by the Acme Company. Your job there was 'accountant.'
Your label is 'accountant.' While you were working, you worked hard, did a good job, probably put money aside and enjoyed the fruits of your labor. Let's call you a **C.**

You are logical, problem solving and literate. This means you can build a logical case in discussing your capabilities with a prospective client.

As you review your personal skill sets and accomplishments, you realize you have done a good job in building a retirement plan for yourself. What if you reconfigured yourself as a financial adviser, helping other people build or handle their retirement accounts? You immediately think of big companies already doing retirement planning and investing: Fidelity Investments, Prudential. Big players. How are you going to go up against them. You can't. Or can You? Blue Sky Time.

What are the liabilities or fears people have in going to one of these commercial giants? They are a small investor. How much individual attention are they going to get? You may understand, but many people don't, some of the terms they use: ROI, Limited Debenture, T-Bills, Munies…Now, who may have the least knowledge, but the greatest need? Think about it. Blue sky it! …Widows 65 and older whose husbands always handled the finances when they were alive.

These women are the most preyed upon by 'friends of the family,' con artists and 'financial advisers' who have their own start-up businesses they want to grow fast. How do these scavengers do so well? They provide 'personal attention.' Women 65 and older have lost many of their personal friends who have moved, gone into nursing homes, or died. They desperately want company and they also need someone they can trust and rely on. Why not you?

Armed with a strong ethical base and a sense of traditional values (also characteristics of a Left Hemisphere person), you apply yourself as a Retirement Advisor for Women 65+.

Your selling premise is that you will be honest, reliable, give personal attention, and ensure their dollars will be invested carefully. You explain hard-to-understand terms in simple language. You go to their house. You keep an individual portfolio to show them how their investments are growing. You protect them from unscrupulous characters trying to separate them from their money. You may build business by referring them to honest attorneys, if they need to update their wills. Those attorneys, in turn, may refer customers to you.

Not only does this provide you with a new career, it re-energizes you.

Example Two:

You didn't reach 45 before you and another fifty secretaries in the building were dismissed. You get together to commiserate and promise to stay in touch. **You and your group are S, socializers. You work best as/in a group.** What is your skill base? Review your past duties. Look at your Left/Right Hemisphere profile. Having trouble placing yourself in one group or the other? You see characteristics in both Left and Right Hemispheres. Absolutely.

Good secretaries utilize both Left and Right Hemispheres.

Your skill base includes multi-tasking, computer proficiency, exceptional phone technique and an abundance of other skills too numerous to mention here.

Your original thought might be working at a Temp Agency. Possible. What else? What are companies doing these days to cut down on staff costs? Off-shoring. Why? Cheaper labor costs. What skills do these people need? Ability to speak English, handle telephones, use computers. What are the start-up costs for these facilities in India, Pakistan, the Philippines? About 130 to $150 million dollars! These costs are expected to be amortized in about three years, thanks to lower wages. **Blue sky it with your friends. How do we use our skill base to match their needs?**

These companies base all their decisions on numbers (Left Hemisphere people). What if we could show them how to eliminate those large start-up costs? What if our start-up costs were $150,000 instead of $130 to150 million? Big savings!

And what if the people were to work at a cost about the same as those foreign counterparts, approximately 60% less than standard wages? Terrific!

And what if these people were in your city so that potential clients didn't have to fly halfway around the world to meet them face to face? Wonderful!

Optimally, you and your friends provide services not just for one company, but for several companies, to offset that lower wage. Your offices are in your homes, with special telephone and internet access. You don't have to fight traffic going in and returning home. You don't have to work every day, nine to five.

That pay cut is not as bad as it looks. You are receiving income from two or three companies, not just one. You eliminate costs of driving, gas, day care, lunches and clothes. Best of all, you don't have someone looking over your shoulder. You don't have to please that manager who doesn't know how to manage.

The reconfiguring you did was to approach companies as a service unit, which saves companies time in recruitment, interviewing and training, providing them with skilled labor at a price competitive to any overseas location.

Example 3:

You are an I personality. In the company you worked for, you were called 'a troubleshooter,' 'Johnny-on-the-spot,' 'the go-to guy.' You have enormous energy and skills. You are the original self-starter. Your problem is unique: you have an abundance of skills.

Your first step is deciding which skills offer you the greatest freedom and profitability. This is a matter of priorities. Let's assume your priorities are something like these:

· be my own boss
· travel
· use my imagination
· meet new people
· make a good living

What you have indicated is that you want to work with several companies at the same time, have varied assignments, and travel. So, you position yourself as an independent agent with a firsthand knowledge of foreign places:

· You are willing to work for a limited time setting up a foreign office.
· You may act as a consultant assessing the risk and potential of opening a market in a certain country.
· You explore whether the country should consider partnering with an existing company in that location.
· You act as a supplier/go-between for an established company.
· You develop contact within the foreign government to ease the company's way into that country.
· You act as a representative for that foreign country to build good relations with American-based companies.

With another organization, say a travel service, you agree to:

· Rate the hotels in a particular area.
· Rate the restaurants.
· List special places to go, things to see.
· Assemble a list of reliable service providers in that area: banks, clothiers, dry cleaners, delivery services, messengers, pharmacies open all night, local shipping services, tailors, etc.

With another organization, you agree to write travel articles and take quality photographs for their magazine.

But don't big companies have these kinds of people on staff already? Maybe or maybe not. Remember, big companies are cutting back on staff and outsourcing to people who aren't asking for medical benefits or retirement benefits.

Or you may target small or mid-sized companies without enormous resources but who are eager to reach the global market and need a knowledgeable, affordable individual who will advise them or act as their early contact.

These three examples are just that…examples. You may already be three jumps ahead of me in applying your personal knowledge and skill base in seeing new applications for your known skills. Good for you!

16

Some Success Stories

Bill K.

Bill was 26 when we first met. He had been working as an apprentice in a company that specialized in developing new polymer mixes for rock guitars. He worked on weekends and was making $400 per weekend.

Now I know as much about polymers and rock performers as your average guy, which means next to nothing. The closest I came to that area was waving at a friendly guy who had offices next to a restaurant I frequented. One early evening he passed my table and paused to chat. My daughter was with me. Some pleasantries were exchanged. When he and his co-workers left, my daughter asked, "How do you know him?"

"Nice guy, isn't he?" I asked. "Dad," she said, "that's Steven Tyler."

Bill K is an S and I personality. Clearly by now he was in a dead-end situation. I asked if he had any particular skills outside what he was doing. "I like to design new guitar shapes and colors." He showed me six drawings he had made. "Ever been in touch with any top stars?" I asked. He had.

I suggested he send these off to the performer and ask him if he knew where there might be a company interested in his skills. He did. Three weeks later he called me from a company in Los Angeles. "They're offering me $40,000 to work for them. What should I say?" "Tell them you'll think about it." (This was in 1990. Today's salary would be about three to five times that amount.) He next called me from San Francisco. "They're talking about $45,000." "Say you'll think about it," I told him.

Bill ultimately chose to work for a guitar company in Connecticut because he wanted to be close to Boston.

So Bill went from an apprenticeship at $400 a week to being a designer at $40,000 a year.

The point of this story is simple. He didn't send out résumés. He didn't even know the name of the companies who called him (and paid his expenses to fly to Los Angeles). He let the right job find him.

John V.

John is a C and S personality. He was working as a pickup driver for a small restaurant. Tired of working for a modest salary and knowing his specialty was desserts, I suggested he draw up a marketing plan to put realistic dimensions on becoming a specialty baker.

He estimated start-up costs and got a bank loan to finance his enterprise. At my suggestion, he visited many upscale restaurants on the South Shore of Boston as well as fine dining establishments in Boston. He asked what their most popular desserts were and the cost of getting them from specialty bakers in the area.

John then found a bakery that had just gone out of business. He put an option to buy on the small plant. With this as a base, he recruited friends to work for him who he knew were reliable and capable. He told them salaries would be low, but as the business grew so would their paychecks.

His marketing plan was simple. He would undercut competitive costs and arrange for faster deliveries (specialty desserts have a short shelf life).

Two years later, as I was leaving a supermarket, John ran up and gave me a bear hug. "I've opened two new bakeries! Three more delivery trucks! Business is booming!"

James S.

James is an C and S personality. He contacted me after reading an article about my Career Counseling in a local newspaper. Jim was employed as a consultant for a large telecommunications company. He enjoyed working for the company but was troubled about his iffy status, each contract running for about four to six months. "I never know if they are going to hire me again and I've got a son and daughter going off to college soon." Jim is a good example of an Intrepreneur, that is, someone who works in a company but must show his worth as an ongoing employee. He tested 28/12 in Left/Right Hemispheres.

"How do I prove my long-term worth to this company?" was a question that came up often. He described his skill sets as writing, being able to analyze reports, adjust to a wide spectrum of situations and settings, and speaking to small and large groups of people to improve their performance and motivate them.

In short, Jim was a very capable manager, but had issues with self-esteem and an unwillingness to seek other career paths. My list of new suggested career paths were:

a. Systems Analyst

b. Motivational speaker

c. Team organizer

d. Seminar Leader

e. Instructor/Teacher

f. Guidance Counselor

g. Event Organizer

h. Public Relations

i. Writer of Program Manuals

Jim read the list and agreed to most of the suggested careers as being "entirely possible." "But I don't want to change direction," he said at last. "I just want to keep working at what I'm doing now but on a regular basis, not as a contract employee."

Back to Square One.

What I suggested he do was talk with some of the top echelon bosses who knew his value and could act as important supporters of his long-term worth. I asked for the names of the top brass and suggested he call them with a simple question: "What do you foresee as long-term problems for this company?" His query raised several important issues (that he had already predicted in his conversations with me).

"Why don't you suggest you work on various 'what-if' scenarios with a firm contract?" I then role-played his conversations with the people he had named.

He would contact me every week to fill me in on discussions he had had with the top brass. I would then suggest various questions he ask next.

Our conversations went on for two months. They stopped when Jim said, "I don't think I need to talk with you anymore. Things are looking good."

Conversations stopped. Objective realized.

Judy C.

Judy was first a student of mine in a class called "Small Business Entrepreneurship." She was 43. "I'm a tax preparer for a large company," she said. "I have people who insist on me every season."

"Why don't you set up your own shop?" I asked her. "I have a non-compete clause in my contract," she said. "For how long?" I asked. "One year," was her answer.

The non-compete clause in her contract said she could not solicit business. "Don't solicit them," I suggested. "If they call you of their own volition, you aren't violating the contract."

They did. She has been working eight years on her own, supporting herself and her husband who was dismissed from his job. Recently she called and said, "I'm tired of this job. It's too seasonal. And I want to do something different."

She and I are working on her next career. With her skill sets I have already identified her next career directions. They are:

a. Interior decorating

b. Financial Advisor

c. Office Manager for an Attorney (a personal friend).

d. Home health care scheduler

e. Manager of Health Care for a local hospital.

f. Human Resource Manager.

g. Sales Representative for tanning salons (a personal friend is trying to
   grow his business).

Judy is already pursuing leads and getting ready for the current tax season. I have suggested she ask none of her friends for a job, rather that she simply schedule for an 'Information Session.'

Even with my reservations about **LinkedIn,** some have suggested that recruiters may use it to look for potential hires. It may be worth a chance.

Some also suggest **Craig's List**. A friend of my did find work as a limo driver with this service and he is sixty-five. He alerted me to the possibilities that 'scam artists' troll this sight and can be deceitful in their postings. He was asked to send money to a particular site and did. He did not get a job, but lost five hundred dollars in the hoped for promise.

Any on-line service has the potential for fraud. I still think face to face contacts are the best way to go. Scammers never appreciate being seen or talking candidly about their operation.

17

<u>From Bartender to Hospital Manager</u>

Debbie L is 53, married and the mother of four children, ages 19, 21, 27, and 29. She is an only child born in Flushing, New York. Her parents divorced when she was two. Her mother was an airline stewardess and Debbie spent nearly all her formative years in Catholic boarding schools. She is an S and I personality. Here is her story:

"My mother pushed me to go to college, a Catholic school in Brookline (Massachusetts). I was really unfocused at the time and I rebelliously quit and got married. The mindset then was that women had four career choices: secretary, nurse, teacher or nun. None of those appealed to me.

My husband and I moved to California, lived in 'The Valley' and then Huntington Beach. I waitressed for a while at Victoria Station and the Black Angus restaurant . I'd done that in high school and college and then I became a bartender. I didn't have a lot of skills but I am very social and would probably talk to the wall if I could.

All my jobs have come through contacts, things that just happened, or friends. I've never answered an ad. I liked bartending because of the social contacts.

My skill sets? I basically like people, which makes me pretty good at getting them to do things without telling them what to do. I'm good at sizing people up, listening to them and prioritizing things. I am also very determined and when I decide to do something, I do it. Some people call me stubborn, so you can take that either way.

My husband's family is from the Boston area, so we came back here in the 80s. I picked up a bartending job at the Plymouth Yacht Club and worked there from 1981 to 1989.

That got kind of old…you can only hear the same stories so many times. But my next job came through a bar customer, a woman who worked at MPG (a newspaper syndication company). This job was selling advertising space. Something I did okay with, but I just didn't really like.

With my nursing major at Northeastern University, I decided to go back to school. I didn't want to waste all those credits. And I had been a biology major for two years at St. Michaels. I finished school.

There was a lot of competition to get into a hospital. They weren't hiring at the time or they were just hiring experienced nurses. There was a freeze on hiring. But a number of doctors and nurses were members of the Yacht Club and I asked around.

Someone put in the word for me. I got hired. You really have to call the person who is hiring directly.

I'm currently the Director of the Telemetry Unit. This job pays more. But I'd really rather help people than sit in meetings all day and do payroll. So I will be returning to my clinical leader role as soon as they find someone. I like to say 'I can be bought,' but really (job) satisfaction is the most important thing.

I haven't seen any age discrimination in nursing but only because there is such a shortage. I have seen it in most other professions. My husband strongly believes that's what happened to him. He was 48, there one day, gone the next. Same thing has happened to a lot of people we know. In his (husband's) case, it really hit him, hurt him a lot. He spent a long time out of work trying to get back into something like he was doing. And just nothing.

Finally I said to him, "You're good with your hands, why don't you try something with that?" We had fixed up old houses and put them back on the market. And he said, "I don't think there's any money in that." But I said, "Give it a try."

Well, he has done very well at that. He's had to hire other people and that's become his new career. And he is doing very, very well at that, thank God, with four children going into college."

Analysis

"All my jobs have come through contacts, things just happened or through friends. I've never answered an ad." What Debbie has done is 'social networking,' which simply means talking to people who might be able to help her find a job and using their leverage to get her placed.

Among her important skills are her sociability and ease in talking with people. She is good at listening, sizing people up and prioritizing tasks: all needed skills in managing people. She has the ability to interact on a one-to-one level, i.e. "I basically like people, which makes me pretty good at getting them to do things without telling them what to do."

She also shows determination and focus. She does not give up in reaching her goal. ("Some people call that stubborn.") **Notice her range of occupations using the same skill sets: bartender, advertising seller, nurse, clinical leader, director of telemetry.**

How far do you think she would have gotten in her nursing career if she had kept the label 'bartender' slapped on her?

18

Secrets for a Successful Job Interview

The interview! The dreaded job interview! If you find job interviews the toughest part of applying for a job, you are not alone. Everyone, including seasoned veterans, admit that nerves are on high alert when the interview takes place. Good news! Interviewers themselves feel less than secure. Why? Their responsibility to the company depends on finding the best person who not only has the needed skills, but will be a 'good fit' inside the company.

Your job as a potential candidate is to make the interviewer feel comfortable; confident in reviewing your credentials, in exploring your personal characteristics, in determining how successful you will be if hired. Don't forget, the interviewer's capabilities will be measured by those to whom he/she reports. Their ability to select the right candidate for employment, has much to say about their capabilities as manager, problem solver, and their powers of observation and decision making..

What generates fear in both the candidate and interviewer? The answer to that question has two parts: situation anxiety and personal anxiety. These fears go back to childhood. Let me explain these terms.

Situation Anxiety:

Remember when you were asked to perform as a kid, before parents, relatives, audiences in the school play. Performance anxiety draws on the ability to shine in a new situation: your adrenalin goes up, your mouth gets dry, your body is on full alert. Perform! Don't let anybody down! How you felt then, how things went (successful/not so successful) are recorded in your memory bank. All those feelings come back unconsciously in an interview.

Being in a new place, the interviewer's headquarters, elicits feelings you associate with being in a new city, or being on a tightrope with hundreds watching. A sense of well being is counteracted by the tension you felt as a child on the street, hanging onto Dad's hand, so you wouldn't get separated or lost. The fight or flight mechanism kicks in, a natural outcome of our brain's wiring.

How do you overcome this? Close your eyes, take several deep breaths, think of a favorite place when you were on vacation. Visualize that scene in your mind's eye. Shake your hands energetically from the wrist. This releases body tension. Don't lock your hands together, let them hang at your sides. This breaks the tension circuit that goes through you with hands locked together.

If your mouth is dry, gently bite the tip of your tongue. It starts salivary juices flowing.

Get to the interview session early. If you don't know the area well, visit that location the day or several days before the interview. Find out where parking is nearby. You want to be calm, cool and collected before the interview begins.

Make sure your appearance is professional: hair cut, shoes shined, white shirt, suit and clean shaven.. If you have a favorite tie or blouse, wear it. For women, blouse appropriate to skirt and jacket, no cleavage, medium heel. (I will not belabor this point. Women over twenty-five instinctively know how to dress). If you really want to know what to wear, go to the place before the interview and look at what others are wearing. Most receptionists will understand and be helpful.

On the day of the interview take time to look at the people who work there. You may gain some important cues about the place. If you're experienced enough, you can watch people's 'body language.' If people move about quickly, head down, you know this is a company that has 'top down' management where the senior executives allow only limited participation to intrude on their thinking. Such companies are rooted to a system invented in 1817, called 'scientific management.' It has the old mindset associated with factory work where managers took the top floor for their offices to get away from the noise below. It is also where the terms, 'upper management, middle management and workers' originally were coined.

In such companies, there is always a 'dress code,' and people speak in hushed voices as if afraid they may be overheard or reported on.

If the employees seem more relaxed, chatting in small groups, this is a 'middle management' organization, sometimes referred to as a 'family company.' Everyone knows who's in charge, but they have more freedom to come up with ideas and let their real personalities show. There will be more individuality in dress and more animation in conversation. Generally speaking, these companies and their policies about pregnancy leave, health care and 401K systems will be more generous.

If people wear dissimilar clothing, speak in a normal tone of voice, you have entered into a team oriented work place. Ideas flow freely bottom to top and teams are based on ability and judged on output. Promotions are based on performance rather than 'the old boy network,' which is to be found in the 'factory mentality, top down' management style.

When you are called back for a second or third interview the manager may say, "it's okay to dress casually, everyone around here does." Follow their lead.

Personal Anxiety: This grows out of our memory and presents itself with the feeling, 'God, I hope I don't screw up!' The feeling of not being good enough is a carry-over from childhood. It may also be expressed with the feeling 'if they really knew me, I wouldn't be here!'

Again, think of yourself as an adult now, not a child. You have valuable gifts to offer the right manager and company. You have earned self respect. Show that in your walk, tone and energy. Tempered enthusiasm in the interview presents you as a professional who knows their worth and is willing to share it with a company who knows what it needs.

Before the Interview, do your homework. Read trade magazines, on-line reviews, talk with knowledgeable friends. Where does this company stand against its competitors? What plans do they have for the future? How do they hope to outdistance rivals in the regional or global market? What kind of people are they looking for to make a meaningful difference?

As you prepare for the interview, write down specific questions to ask the decision maker. Be sure and ask them. This shows your interest in this specific company. Remember you are not just looking for a job, you are looking for meaningful work that will ignite your passions and fully use your skills.

You have as much at stake as the person who conducts the interview. Don't forget that.

Interviews fall into predictable patterns. They are:

- **Small talk**
- **Tell me about yourself**
- **Let's look at your resume**
- **Why do you think you'd be right for this position?**
- **Questions, wrap-up, handshake, elevator**

So let's go through each of these steps to show you at your best.

Small Talk

Sometimes called 'the ice breaker,' these few minutes are usually solicitous on the interviewer's part. Questions like "Have any trouble with traffic?" or "Would you like some coffee?" These questions are meant to put the applicant at ease. Politely refuse the coffee: you may spill it on your papers or show your hand is shaking. It is also the interviewer's first full length view of you. Again, stand straight, show a smile and look about the interviewer's office for anything that reveals their character.

Family photo? "Attractive family. That taken on your vacation?" Or seeing a photo of a marlin catch with interviewer standing next to the fish. "Wow, that must have been an experience! How big was that marlin? How long did it take to bring him on board?" If you are an avid fisherman, you might add, "I love fishing…but I've never caught anything that size!"

What you're doing here is creating a personal connection, as well as showing you are attentive and have an eye for detail.

How were you brought to the manager's office? Did his secretary tell you the way or escort and announce you? If you were just pointed in the right direction, this is probably early in the interview process, which is sometimes referred to as 'the cattle call.' If you were escorted, it generally means your reputation has gotten favorable attention and you may be a prime candidate or that a friend has used their influence to arrange the meeting.

The secretary/receptionist should have announced you by telephone. If the interviewer/manager is on his/her phone, back turned to you, some managers use this ploy to show how important they are, do not hover in the doorway. Seat yourself, preferably at the table with chairs or on the couch. What this says is that you are not intimidated or frightened.

Seating yourself helps send the signal you are as important as the manager. If the manager keeps his/her back to you, but waves you to a chair in front of his/her desk, it will probably be too close to the desk, making you squirm your way into the seat. Pull the chair out. If it faces a glaring window, turn the chair so the 'important manager' has to look into the brightness. All of this nonsense is part of a mystique started in the 1980s when it was called 'Power Furniture" or some other fashionable name.

Seating arrangements play a significant role. If you are motioned to a small round table with chairs, let the manager sit and choose the seat one apart and to the right. If you are motioned to a couch, this is a better indication that you are a prime candidate.

Tell Me About Yourself:

The interviewer is moving from small talk to an open-ended question to gain a general sense of how you see yourself. Now is the time to position yourself to best advantage.

"I have excellent management skills. That's not just my opinion, but what others have said about me. I'm good at getting the best out of people who report to me. I'm very good at communication, verbally and in writing. What other information might be helpful to you?"

What you are doing is narrowing the funnel to see what the manager considers most important.

Key here is to keep the interview a dialogue, not just a question and answer session. Questions given to the interviewer help keep the dialogue flowing and ascertaining exactly what the interviewer considers important skills/qualities that will make you absolutely right for the job.

Remember, you have as much at stake here as the manager asking the questions. One of the best ways to maximize your input are questions like these:

1. Ask the person how long they have worked at the company

2. Ask this person how they find the working environment. Is it 'by the book', or is some imagination and personal contribution welcomed and rewarded?

3. Ask the interviewer how they happened to land here? What is their background?

4. Ask the interviewer to tell you more about what the company is looking for, what immediate and long range goals are hoping to be achieved with candidate selection.

5. Make a comment such as, "I want to be sure I'm the right person for this job. Believe me, I'll be the first person to tell you if this doesn't sound like a good fit."

Occasionally write down something the interviewer has said. It indicates you are listening carefully and that the other person has said something worth writing down. You may refer back to this later by saying, "You made a point about X that I thought was very interesting…Could we talk a bit more about that?"

Mirroring the interviewer's body language is always a good idea. Sales people learn this technique early on. If the interviewer leans forward when making an important point, you do the same.

Maintain eye contact for about five seconds at a time. Picking up on key words and repeating them back also helps build rapport. All this indicates you are a good listener, that you are attentive, that you really want this job.

Answer questions but keep the answer open ended. Political candidates do this all the time. Keep stressing your strong points: I'm very quick at picking things up…and I'm very good with people."

A specific question may lead you to refer to something illustrative in your résumé. This gives validation to your answer.

Never say anything negative about a previous employer. If you were fired, don't mention it. Your previous employer will give no specific information other than to say how long you were with the company.

The more the interviewer talks about him/herself, the more likely the interviewer will give you high marks.

The interviewer needs to be able to give solid evidence for why you are being recommended or hired to their superiors. Giving the interviewer confidence in their decision to hire you, makes them your best advocate in discussing you.

"What would you say are your weaknesses?" This a favorite question interviewers like to ask.

The best answer you can give is to say something like, "I'm something of a perfectionist. I always feel whatever I do could be better. I try not to impose those standards on other people too much, because it's a personal thing. If other people sense my standards, I think they try and emulate them".

Let's Look at Your Resume:

Every month some 'expert' comes up with a new design for how a résumé should be formatted. This is done primarily to generate work for résumé companies. Here are some simple tips on how to organize yours:

- Re-write your résumé specifically for the job you are seeking. Make sure it is up-to-date. Write it to point strongly to those areas the decision maker has indicated are important to success here.

- Use whatever 'buzz words' or 'technical jargon' used in your first information interview, if you had one. Companies love describing themselves in current clichés; i.e. 'cutting edge', 'pushing the envelope', 'innovative', 'ground breaking,' 'forward looking,' etc. Don't overdo them, of course.

- Job titles are not as important as results of your actions. Use action words that describe the outcome of what you have accomplished in your previous position, such as 'reduced operating costs by 82 million dollars', or 'created programs that upgraded company skill levels to world class standards.' By way of example let's look at two versions of the same job description:

Warehouse Supervisor: Responsible for managing daily operations: space allocation, running inventory, maintenance of equipment, supervision of 120 workers.
or
Warehouse Manager: Supervising 120 people, redesign of space allocation, resulting in 20% more storage area and better entry/exit of all vehicles. Increased capacity resulted in $2.4 million greater profit. Redesign eliminated 12% of equipment needed, with annual savings of $1.2 million. Improved lighting that reduced worker injury by 12% and lowered insurance policy by $500,000. Instituted worker incentive program to improve morale, safety and increased productivity. Citation from President James Clements on savings, worker performance and team management.

Now, which resume description do you think presents you in a more favorable light and enhances your chance of being hired? Always shape your resume along these objective measures, spelling them out in detail and showing dollar savings or increased team management as the final result of your talents and dedication.

- Print your résumé on heavy weight, quality paper, either white or cream. Have a copy for yourself as well as the interviewer. Use it to lead the interviewer through 'talking points' that show you in the best possible light.

- List additional skills such as mastery with Excel, Power Point, One Note, Outlook. etc.

- List hobbies that apply to job related functions. The interviewer is not interested in your fishing or bowling skills.

- Copy any newspaper articles or work related prizes you have received, or anything that illustrates recognition outside your previous employer. Feel free to discuss why you gained personal satisfaction from the prize or article. With modesty, of course.

If you have had several careers, only list those relevant to the interview. (I have five separate résumés as professor, motivational speaker, voice over announcer, business history, president of my own company).

List your education degrees. You need not supply the year you graduated. This sums up most of what you need to know on résumés. Let's move on.

A specific question may lead you to refer to something illustrative in your résumé. Use your resume as evidence you are right for this job. This gives validation to your answer.

The more the interviewer talks about him/herself, the more likely the interviewer will feel good about you. Giving the interviewer confidence in their decision to hire you, makes them your best advocate in discussing you.

For great advice on answering Interview Questions, I suggest you go to this website: **about.com guide jobs**

Questions/Wrap-up:

It is entirely appropriate to ask when a decision will be made. This suggests you may be looking at other companies. It is also helpful to ask, "Any other questions you'd like to ask? I'd like to be sure I've given you a good picture of who I am and make you comfortable in recommending me for this position."

Acknowledge the secretary on your way out. "It was good meeting you. I hope to see you again," is always appropriate.

Many bosses will ask their secretary, 'What did you think of this guy?' Eliciting a positive response on their part is always a good conclusion to the interview.

If the interviewer walks you to the elevator, you can be sure the meeting went well.

Never ask about salary at this meeting. Never suggest references to the interviewer. If they want them, they will ask.

We'll talk about salary negotiation and references in the next chapter.

19

References, Salary Negotiations and Contracts

References are again simple verifications that you are the qualified candidate you presented in your interview. Give the interviewer the names of people you have worked with or some recognizable leader in the business community who knows you.

Be sure the names you supply are good, reliable friends. (Avoid someone on the make who may give you a lukewarm response, hoping they may have a chance to get the job if they don't praise you warmly).

Contact your references as quickly as possible after the interview. Tell them who may be calling and the specific things you want them to stress. These are the points you made in the interview: wonderful manager, great with people, fair in your judgments, an encouraging boss willing to share credit with the people who worked for him, etc.

It is important for your references to play up these points quickly because the interviewer's call will probably last only a few minutes. Again, what the interviewer is doing is validating and re-affirming their interview takeaway. It is simple reassurance they can pass on to their supervisor.

The next question you'll want to ask yourself is 'Do I want to work inside the company or act as an Outside Contractor?'

There is no right or wrong answer to this question. It's all a matter of gut feel. Some people are more secure working inside a company with the assurance of a weekly or monthly paycheck coming in. If the company offers any kind of additional benefits, picking up some of your health plan costs, this may be an important deciding factor, especially if your spouse does not have coverage or you are a single parent.

Generally speaking, C and S types will feel more secure inside a company setting.

Be aware if you are hired on a part-time basis, which is increasingly the case, you will not be eligible for health care or any other benefits. Factor that thinking into your salary negotiations.

If, on the other hand, you work as an Independent Contractor, say as a consultant, you have the leverage to work for several other companies at the same time, as long as both companies do not work in the same specialized field. There your participation may be seen as a 'conflict of interest.' You may work at a negotiated rate (per assignment) or on a monthly retainer.

In your favor, the company will have to sign a contract spelling out your duties, hours assured, for a specific time period. Always get it in writing!

You may have the freedom to work off company premises. Maintaining a private home office offers many tax benefits. Whether you decide to pay taxes each month or on a yearly basis is something you should discuss with a good tax attorney.

You also have a good deal more predictability in how long the assignment runs because you are now working on a contractual basis. If the company you are working with hits a downturn, they may layoff a part-timer. The same can't happen to you. You have a binding contract.

If you are an I personality, you will probably seek work as an Independent Contractor.

If you are still working for a company that is undergoing successive firing waves, you may wish to explore the possibilities of working as an Independent Contractor before the axe falls. You will be doing essentially what you are doing now or perhaps take on an additional function that will save the company more dollars. (Be clear that you are not willing to give up any benefits such as 401ks you may have earned as a full time employee).

If you see many of your associates being fired and you are still employed, put out feelers to your company's biggest competitor and offer your services there. (There's always something that appeals to a company's ego in hiring away someone from their competition).

Or you may start sending out discreet signals to business associates at other companies, telling them you are considering a move and to keep their ears open.

The best time to get a job is while you still have a job.

Let me here mention a reality of today's marketplace. Many companies, especially Fortune 500 companies, are arbitrarily firing people when they hit ages 40-43. This has nothing to do with performance on your part. It is an actuarial decision. Some bean counter you never met has projected your salary and retirement benefits. Or you have reached some numerical grade level no one ever mentioned that puts a ceiling on your pay.

You may be terminated, or as some companies like to delicately put it, 'your position has been discontinued'.

The likelihood of getting your same job at another company is possible, but not likely. Other Fortune 500 companies will probably have the same mindset as your previous employer.

Does this decrease in income always hold true? No, it doesn't. If you land a job in certain industries, which we'll discuss later, you may find your income will increase anywhere from 20 to 30%. (Go back and look at Lea M. mentioned in Chapter Two, whose salary increased by $11,000). She picked a work category where there is an expanding field of opportunities. It proves the old adage, 'Find a need and fill it.'

Your future career should be to something you enjoy, something that will rekindle your passion for work and recharge your energy. As one of my savvy friends remarked, "The best thing that ever happened to me was getting fired from the _____company. I finally got to do what I loved and I no longer had to deal with a room full of monkeys."

I personalities will recognize their fullest potential in today's marketplace. But C personalities and S types will find they have more talents than they realize and their skills are valued by smaller companies who value those 40+. You bring a wealth of knowledge and demonstrated skills to companies who value expertise and are willing to pay for it.

Those entering the work force with new Master's Degrees are discovering that many companies are not so impressed. While these fresh young faces believe they should be given high level positions because of their degrees, they face a different kind of hurdle. They don't have a proven work record.

My advice to those recently graduated is to get into the workforce as quickly as possible. You have the energy and the up-to-date skills employers want and need. No one starting out is going to be hired simply because of a degree. All graduates are not equal. Those who are best at networking and willing to work at a salary that may not be as high as expected, will probably find their degree works in their favor long term.

Salary negotiation still exists. When the job is offered, you may be so glad to get it you accept the amount offered. My recommendation is to ask some pertinent questions of the manager offering you the job:

1. <u>Do you have any latitude in this position on salary?</u>

Most companies have a dollar range connected with the job, say $70,000 to $76,000. You will be offered the lowest figure. If the company really wants you, they may adjust the amount upwards.

Don't forget the manager you're talking with has been through a long process of interviewing candidates. This has been an additional burden on them. They still have their daily duties to perform. It is worth the adjustment up in pay to retain you.

2. <u>Ask about any additional benefits that may sweeten the deal from your vantage point.</u>

While health and retirement benefits are off the table, perhaps the company will offer you a company car, especially if your assignment requires a good deal of 'field work,' driving to various accounts some distance away.

3. <u>Working from home at least several days a week is another question to raise.</u>

Single parents with a child will find this to be a valuable option: less money for child care, more time to spend with your child. Companies benefit too with this arrangement. They don't have to use expensive office space. Again, remember the value of setting up a home office. There are special tax advantages that you may deduct each year for electric, heating, depreciation on office equipment, trash collection, etc. Find a good tax preparer who can walk you through all the legitimate deductions.

Entering the workforce has never been easy. I speak from experience here. But the skills you learn in any work area are transferable to your next career. That is what this book is all about. Consider work experience and what you learn from any job as money in your memory bank.

Recognize your value. Adaptability is key. Aptitudes allow you to shuffle the cards and win at the game. App yourself!

20

Entrepreneurship

Entrepreneurs are people who turn a hobby into a career. C,S and I people have a good chance at being successful at this. If you look back at the sections on 'what are your hobbies?' or 'what are your passions,' you will see that your hobbies provided genuine satisfaction not found in your nine- to- five occupation. You used it as an outlet for creative juices not allowed by your then current job.

You have probably spent a good many years at your hobby, researching it, becoming proficient at it, staying passionate about it. So now, it's your turn to turn that hobby into a paying proposition.

'How do I get started?' is the usual question. Well, first you may need 'seed money.' This means your initial start-up dollars. If your credit card balances are routinely paid, the start-up money can come from there. So can a bank loan on your house. Keep the word 'minimal' in mind. Work up a good estimate on start-up costs. If this is all new to you, use the resources on line by going to www.sba.gov The Small Business Administration will help you discover the ins and outs of initial funding, the tax laws you need to know for your particular state and even provide a short personality test to help you discover if you have the patience and stamina connected with successful entrepreneurship

One of the easiest ways to get started is to buy into an existing business and eventually gain full equity in the business. 'Sweat equity' means you work there, taking what would be your salary and paying it forward to eventual ownership. Older owners may see this as a real opportunity and enjoy teaching you the 'insider' tricks of the trade.

The key to your own successful start-up is to think of it as a business, not a hobby. You must survey the competition in your area, or if you are thinking of an on-line product or service, your first question to yourself is answering the simple statement: 'What value do I offer in this area others don't?'

Let me step into my familiar role of Professor of Marketing and Advertising and give you a very short lesson.

You have four areas of advantage in marketing your product or service. They are:

- **performance**
- **packaging**
- **price**
- **place**

Let me briefly explain. If you outclass everybody with product or service performance, you can charge the highest price allowable and people will buy it. Performance is buttressed by price. The thinking here is 'you get what you pay for. Quality costs more.'

If you aren't the leader in performance, you can succeed with packaging. Packaging means you bundle services: you do this and also that, and that too. You reinforce your image with a lower price than the top performer.

Price works both ways: establishing higher quality: 'Only from Neiman-Marcus' or lower price: 'Why pay more?' Amazon. com. Both establish price and place as synonymous with value.

In selling yourself there is one secret to success: differentiation. You must set yourself apart from all competitors in your category by stating clearly what you provide others don't. If you can't make this claim and prove it, you have little chance of success.

Earlier in this book, I gave the example of becoming a personal financial advisor to women whose husbands have died, responsibility for handling personal wealth now on their shoulders. I pointed out that the big companies, Chase, Fidelity Investments, Charles Schwab are big, fairly impersonal companies. Offering personal services and going to the person's house is the key to a more individualized approach.

This example suggests that many services may be offered to those of advanced years: shopping, cleaning, meal preparation, driving people to and from doctor's appointments, simple tasks that require little in the way initial investment and providing you with personal satisfaction.

The aging population provides an enormous range of opportunities for you to fill.

Equally, with working families, chances for you to house sit pets or provide day care for children of working mothers are useful, fulfilling and relatively inexpensive ways to become a service provider.

If your hobby is golf or tennis, you might think of becoming an instructor to those just starting the sport or who wish to become better players.

Starting your own fabric design business, help with interior decorating, working with thrift shops to find customer bargains, all of these roles keep start-up costs to a minimum.

The real key in all this is doing what you know and love and making some money doing it.

Network with friends, offer services you can post on bulletin boards in your local supermarket, go on-line with a website, take out a small ad in your community newspaper: all these provide outlets for your talents and getting the word out inexpensively.

Decide how much time you wish to devote to your own small business. Even those still working may find this a satisfying outlet. Blue sky it with friends. Don't just think of it as making more money, but rather sharing your personal gifts with others. All this will help give you greater satisfaction and a sense of independence, and help pay the bills. Think big…and think small!

21

Company Size and Growth Opportunities

While Fortune 500 companies have been shedding jobs, small businesses have been hiring. Small business by definition means companies with fifteen to five hundred employees. While they may be described as small, their impact on the American economy is enormous. *Statistics supplied by the SBA Office of Advocacy, created by Congress in 1976. For more information visit the website, www.sba.gov/advocacy/847.

Small business represents 99.7% of all employer firms.

Small business employs 44% of all private sector employees.

Small business has generated 65% of net new jobs over the past 17 years.

In 2009, there were 27.5 million small businesses in the United States. They employ about half of all U.S. workers.

Small firms accounted for 65% of the fifteen million new jobs created between 1993 and 2009.

Small business also makes up 97.5% of all identified exporters and produced 31% of export value in FY 2008.

Small business produced 13 times more patents per employee than large companies!

Small business, indeed!

And what is the common complaint among all these small business companies?

Finding new employees who are experienced.

What qualities are sought by small business? These are the traits most often mentioned:

1. Generalists: This means people who know a lot about a lot of things. Where large companies push for specialization in one area (remember the constraints of your old job description) generalists are people adept in several areas. This frees them up to work with others, contribute more, multitask and become team players.

2. Good Communicators: Being able to write and speak coherently, make ideas clear, allowing others to bring their thinking to a project, listen carefully, reduce seemingly complex issues to basic essentials. Good communicators make use of eye contact, body language, rough sketches, to share what is in their head with others in vivid, concrete terms.

3. Enthusiasm: This means bringing energy, inspiration, zeal, 'out of the box thinking' and excitement to the work at hand. It means involving others in solving a problem or looking ahead into the future. Enthusiasm is contagious and makes for more dynamic individuals and groups. This quality makes people look forward to work, enhancing self-esteem and a positive work ethic.

4. Quick learner: Adaptability, flexibility, picking up on ideas and systems in a shortened time frame are the attributes of a quick learner. This dovetails nicely with good communication, generalist capabilities and enthusiasm. Every day may be a learning experience and allow people to bring new ideas and insights to the table.

5. Responsible for getting things done: A sense of mastery plays a large role in making workers feel they 'own' a project. Instead of submitting ideas and waiting months for some unseen 'big shot' to agree, disagree or otherwise comment, getting things done quickly and right the first time helps build confidence, individualism and pride in a small company. It also helps management see who the real performers are.

Isn't this the kind of place you want to join?

There are also more rewards inherent in small business. In a small company you may be interviewed by the ultimate decision maker, the owner of the business.

Decisions are made quickly. You will know that day or a few days later whether or not the job is yours.

More good news: you are much more visible in a small business. Small business pays for performance. Some companies offer a hiring bonus. Others may reward your dedication and performance with incentive bonuses.

Small business pays more often for health benefits and stock options, meaning that as the company grows, your nest egg grows with it. Remember Microsoft when it was still a small company. Many employees became millionaires by getting in on the ground floor before Microsoft became a worldwide giant. Bill Gates actually attends parties for retirees and congratulates those walking away with a million plus in the bank. He also suggests employees e-mail him with ideas. (http.www.wikipedia.com)

Accessibility to work with the boss creates an atmosphere where everybody wants to shine and you have the chance to catch a piece of the spotlight.

Small business is also the place to go for outsourcing of projects. This may prove to be the door that opens to full time employment.

All personality types, C,S and I can find opportunities with small business.

C people are career oriented, often described as 'having a gift for something.' C people have a career compass that creates total focus on what they do. C people are critical of themselves and their performance. With a specified role and the chance to prove their worth, C people may be a perfect fit for companies that prize energy and focus. Steve Ballmer, Bill Gates' thirtieth employee at Microsoft, began at a salary of $50,000. He is recognized for his energy, devotion to the company, and his skills in operations and sales. He later moved on to become Chief Executive Officer and then President of the company. His net worth as of 2012 was estimated at $15.7 billion dollars.. (httpwww:wikipedia.com)

S people are social animals. They are group oriented. The workplace for them is like an extended family. They are loyal people as well as task-oriented. They thrive in smaller companies where everyone gets to know everyone. They will be quick to recommend friends who might be successful in this new place and may be understood to serve as a 'human resources' person without the overhead of a formal Human Resources Department.

I people are realistic, pragmatic and stimulated by ideas. They excel at working in a team often becoming team leader by common recognition of other team members. They have charisma, have the ability to laugh at themselves and work on many projects simultaneously. Their value to a start-up or small company may be invaluable.

<u>Growth Industries</u>

As our population ages, healthcare opportunities and pharmaceuticals will continue to be expanding industries. Particularly, health care means 'hands-on' workers that cannot be off-shored or downsized. You can't take a patient's temperature or plan meal selection from an office in Pakistan. There are many opportunities in hospitals, senior care, hospice, and other activities that require face to face services.

For those who can't stand the sight of blood, there are many staff administration positions they may be just right for you.

Personal Finance

Knowing where and when to help people invest their savings wisely, and give personal face-to-face attention, is another growth area. Often wary of larger investment firms, personality, as well as professional expertise are valued by many people. This includes young marrieds as well as those facing retirement and widows.

Banking

Your local bank may be an excellent source of new hires. Banks are willing to train and age is not so important a factor. Many banks also serve as financial advisors.

Construction

Construction has hit a slow growth period as building of new homes has bottomed out. But streets, highways and bridges, airports, harbors have all seen deterioration. Veterans of the wars in Iraq, Afghanistan and Pakistan are returning home. They are valuable, given their training to work as a team and their knowledge in many applicable areas of construction. It is only a matter of time before billions will be spent in retrofitting cities and rural areas all around the country. Again, this is an industry that cannot be off-shored or outsourced.

How do I find these opportunities?

In your area, banks are good sources of information on startup companies. They lend them money to get started. Building a good rapport with bank officers who know you, your reputation (and your credit rating), they can help or recommend you to entrepreneurs in local communities.

Newspapers, trade magazines, web sites, even Craigslist may prove helpful in spotting new jobs.

Small companies have found the Web has leveled the playing field with access nationally and globally. Who would have thought a small brewer like Brooklyn Beer would become a high priced, in-demand specialty for business men wooing new clients in Tokyo? A glass of Brooklyn Beer may sell for as high as $150.

Creating a website for yourself is inexpensive and reaches a world-wide audience. Phone apps guide users to virtually any area of interest. Truly App yourself here!

Your local Chamber of Commerce is also a way to gain exposure for your talents. As a guest speaker (without a direct sales approach) you can call attention to your specialty. Writing a local column in a community newspaper is yet another way to sell, without selling.

Believe it or not, another source of job tracking is your local dry cleaning establishment. Nearly everyone uses their services. Many dry cleaners have bulletin boards that allow customers to put up service announcements and 'Needed' postings.

Dry cleaners have become the equivalent of the old 'general store' where folks gathered around a pot bellied stove to get warm and discuss the local news. They welcome customers who provide services and will help you advertise yourself. Supermarkets also have bulletin boards for services offered.

A friend of mine took a 'Needed' telephone number for 'dog walking services'. Today she has her own company and employs three other people.

Possibilities are endless.

Keep looking. Stay positive. Stretch your imagination and find new avenues. Attitude and application of your unique skills is what it's all about. App Yourself!

I wish you much success.

P.S. I'd like to hear to hear your success story after using this book. Let me know how it helped you, what position you had and what you do now. With your permission, I may include it in the next edition of this book.

Contact me at: appyourselfnow@gmail.com